Puerto Rico

Don Philpott

Published by
Landmark Publishing
Ashbourne Hall
Cokayne Avenue, Ashbourne
Derbyshire DE6 1EJ

Published by:
Landmark Publishing Ltd,
Ashbourne Hall, Cokayne Avenue, Ashbourne, Derbyshire DE6 1EJ England
E-mail landmark@clara.net Web-site www.landmarkpublishing.co.uk

ISBN 1 901522 34 2

Print: Gutenberg Press Ltd, Malta
Cartography: Mark Titterton
Design: Mark Titterton

Front cover: Caja Muertos, Ponce
Back Cover top: Old San Juan
Back Cover bottom: Snorkelling , Icacos

Photograph credits: Travel and Sports®, Inc Front Cover, Back Cover top and bottom,
6, 7, 11, 14, 15t, 15b, 31, 34, 35, 39, 43t, 43b, 51, 59, 62, 67t, 71t, 71b. Puerto Rico
Tourism Co. (Bob Krist) 18, 30, 50, 54. SETI Institute and Seth Shastak, 67b,
Title page (Robin Hood), Don Philpott, 18t

Opposite page: A romantic sunse

Puerto Rico

Don Philpott

• CONTENTS •

• FEATURE BOXES •

• MAPS •

*I*ntroduction

GETTING THERE

By air: Puerto Rico's Luis Muñoz Marín International Airport is two and a half hours from Miami, 1,045 miles (1682km), three and a half hours from New York, 1,597 miles (2571km), four and a half hours from Chicago, 2,072 miles (3336km), and seven and a half hours from Los Angeles, 3,401 miles (5476km).

Between them, Air Canada, American Airlines, American Eagle, Delta, United and USAir fly into San Juan from most major North American cities. American Airlines also operates non-stop services from Miami and New York's JFK Airport to Aguadilla, and from Miami to Ponce. San Juan is American Airlines' main Caribbean hub with connecting flights to Europe and Latin America. American Eagle, LIAT and other operators operate scheduled services from San Juan throughout the Caribbean. Carnival Airlines has flights to Aguadilla and Ponce from New York and Newark. There are also scheduled services from Mexico and South America with LACSA and other major airlines. British Airways, Air France, Iberia and Lufthansa operate scheduled services to San Juan from London, Paris, Madrid and Frankfurt.

From Europe you can also fly in via a number of US gateways.

By boat: San Juan is the largest home-based cruise port in the world. Almost 30 cruise ships use San Juan as their homeport, and each year hundreds of cruise ships visit. Most of the main cruise lines visit San Juan.

GEOGRAPHY

The Commonwealth of Puerto Rico, a possession of the United States, lies at the eastern end of the Greater Antilles in the Caribbean Sea. The Commonwealth covers the main island of Puerto Rico and a number of offshore islands including Culebra and Vieques off the east coast, and Mona Island just to the west. The Atlantic Ocean is to the north and the Caribbean to the south.

Puerto Rico is 100 miles (161km) from Hispaniola to the west and 40 miles (64km) from the US Virgin Islands to the east. The US mainland is about 1,000 miles (1,610km) to the northwest.

The island, the easternmost and smallest of the Greater Antilles, is roughly rectangular in shape, about 110 miles (179km) from east to west, and 40 miles (64km) from north to south. Puerto Rico, including the offshore islands, covers an area of 3515 sq. miles (9144 sq.km).

The land is mostly mountainous, and the spine that runs through the island is the ridge of a massive submarine range that runs from Central America across the Caribbean to the Lesser Antilles. The island's highest point is Cerro De Punta 4,389ft (1338m), but off the northern coast of the island, the seabed plunges in a trench to 28,374ft (8647m) - the deepest point in the Atlantic Ocean.

The island is a result of relatively recent geological folding, faulting

Arecibo Lighthouse and Historical Park

and uplift; and this process is still continuing with occasional minor earthquakes.

The **Central Cordillera** is the highest mountain range, with altitudes of more than 4,000ft (1219m). It is in the center of the island, closer to the south coast than the north, with steep slopes rising from the south coast to the summit, and then sloping more gently down to the northern coast. There are a number of large basins in the mountains, the largest of which is the **Caguas Valley**, which provide level land suitable for agriculture, and there is a long narrow stretch of lowland along the northern coastline.

Most of the island's rain falls on the northern slopes and so most of the rivers drain from the center of the island to the north-facing coast. Many of these have been harnessed to provide hydroelectric power, drinking water and water for crop irrigation. Many of the rivers in the southern half of the island are dry for much of the year, except after heavy rain, and farming in the south is only possible with irrigation.

A LITTLE HISTORY

The first settlers are believed to have been Indians from the Florida peninsula who were already in the island by 100BC, although little is known about them. They are believed to have been foragers who lived close to the coast and lived on wild fruit and fish. They were succeeded by the Igneri, skilful potters who established small villages along the coast. Prior to 1000AD Taíno Indians, a sub-group of Arawak Amerindians, arrived after paddling their way north through the Lesser Antilles in

dugout canoes from Venezuela. They called the island BORIKÉN [Boh-Ree-KEN].(This name subsequently mutated into Borinquen)

The Taíno were a peaceful people, who fished, hunted and cultivated plants such as maize, sweet potatoes, tobacco and cassava. They lived in small coastal communities, wore almost no clothes but decorated themselves with tattoos, feathers and beads, and crafted household and religious items from wood, clay, conch, bone and stone. They had a well-developed social system and were led by hereditary chiefs called 'caciques'. Village huts were round or rectangular with reed walls and thatched roofs. Early European records show that they enjoyed dancing, either for pleasure or as part of rituals, and they played ball games. The warlike Caribs, who like the Arawaks were Amerindians from South America, were feared as cannibals. They followed the Arawaks through the Lesser Antilles but they didn't settle in Puerto Rico. The Caribs did raid the island from time to time, but the Arawaks were largely left in peace.

EARLY EXPLORERS

Christopher Columbus did not chance upon Puerto Rico but was led to it during his second Caribbean voyage of discovery by Arawaks. They had been captured during a Carib raiding party on Puerto Rico and were taken to Guadeloupe where the Spanish rescued them. Columbus promised to return them to their island and on 19 November 1493, his 17-ship fleet anchored off the west coast of Puerto Rico. He claimed the island for Spain and called it **San Juan Bautista** (St. John the Baptist). It was to remain in

Spanish hands until 1898. Two days later, the fleet sailed for Hispaniola, where the first European settlement in the New World was established.

In 1508 Juan Ponce de León (who as far as is known did not sail with Columbus in 1493) was granted royal permission to explore the island and appointed the first governor. He established the first settlement slightly inland from the northeast coast and called it Caparra, but it was abandoned in a few years because of mosquitoes. Settlers then moved to an islet beside a large natural harbor, which was named Puerto Rico (rich port). Over the years, the island became known as Puerto Rico while the settlement and then the town that developed was called San Juan.

These first explorers had heard stories of fabulous gold and silver mines on the island, and demanded that the Arawaks not only accept the sovereignty of the Spanish king, but also pay a levy in gold. The Indians were also forced to work for their Spanish masters, and despite their peaceful nature, they finally rebelled in 1511. They were no match for the heavily armed Spanish troops and were quickly defeated and subjugated. It is thought there were about 30,000 and 50,000 Taíno living on the island at the time, but over the next 200 years their numbers were decimated. Many died in slavery and others succumbed to European diseases to which they had no resistance. By the end of the 17th century, there were fewer than 2,000 Taíno on the island.

There were gold deposits on the island, and the Indians were put to work mining them, but they ran out by 1530, and the settlers switched to farming. (Indian were never technically "slaves", but rather "protegés", and African slaves were brought in large numbers later).

Much of the land was unsuitable for agriculture, and most farms were small subsistence holdings. A plantation system was not really introduced until the end of the 19th century when greater numbers of African slaves were introduced.

In the mid- to late-16th century, the island was attacked many times by Carib raiding parties who carried off food and slaves. The Carib war canoes, sometimes paddled by 100 men, were so powerful that they could overtake and attack sailing ships.

TROUBLED TIMES

Puerto Rico was repeatedly attacked by French, English and Dutch Corsairs, and San Germán the island's second settlement, was sacked and destroyed several times.

Realizing the strategic importance of the island, the Spanish fortified San Juan. The impressive fortifications not only protected the harbor approaches but also ringed the town. In 1595 **Sir Francis Drake** attacked San Juan, but could not penetrate the harbor because of cannon fire from the El Morro fortress. In 1598 the Earl of Cumberland successfully attacked the town, but he was forced to leave the island after an outbreak of dysentery among his troops. And, in 1625 the Dutch privateer Bowdoin Hendrik managed to slip into the harbor. His men sacked the town and set fire to it, but they were unable to take the fortress.

Following this attack, the defences were strengthened with the addition of a city wall 25 feet (7.6m) high and 18 feet (5m) thick, making San Juan virtually impregnable.

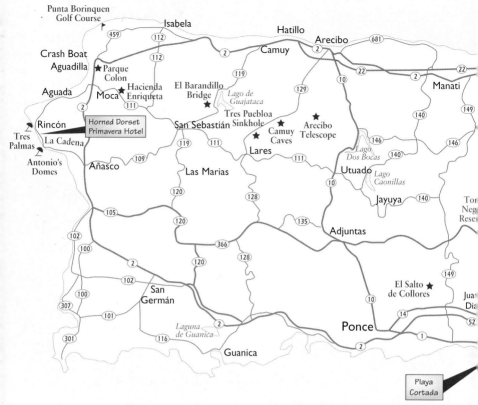

While San Juan became an important port of call, the rest of the country was largely left to its own devices. The farmers grew their crops and traded with passing ships and settlements on neighboring islands. Towards the end of the 18th century, trade between the island and Spain was opened up, and serious efforts were made to boost the island's economy and productivity, and reduce its dependence on Spanish coffers. The move was also necessary because of the rapidly expanding population, up from about 45,000 in 1765 to more than 100,000 in 1780 and over 150,000 by 1800.

Immigration was encouraged and many of the new settlers were farmers with knowledge of large-scale agriculture. Coffee was introduced and the first exports shipped out in 1776. Sugar cane also became an important crop and because it required intensive labor, African slaves were introduced. By 1800, the slave population had risen to more than 13,000.

NAPOLEON

In 1808 Napoleon invaded Spain, incarcerated the Bourbon king Ferdinand V11, and put his brother Joseph Bonaparte on the throne. Many of the Spanish Central and South American colonies used this as an excuse to seek independence. On Puerto Rico, however, the colony remained loyal to the imprisoned king largely because of

PUERTO RICO

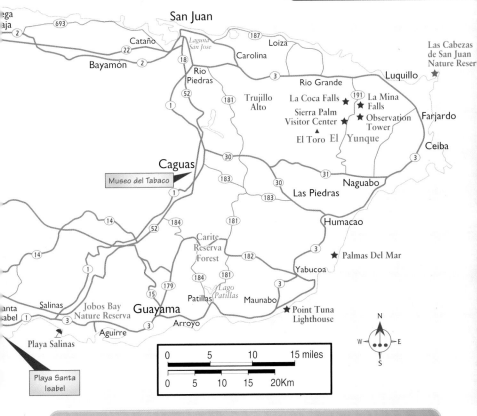

San Juan

Cataño
Bayamón
Rio Piedras
Trujillo Alto
Caguas
Museo del Tabaco
Carolina
Loiza
Rio Grande
Luquillo
Las Cabezas de San Juan Nature Reser
La Coca Falls
La Mina Falls
Sierra Palm Visitor Center
Observation Tower
El Toro
El Yunque
Farjardo
Ceiba
Naguabo
Las Piedras
Humacao
Carite Reserva Forest
Palmas Del Mar
Yabucoa
Lago Patillas
Maunabo
Salinas
Jobos Bay Nature Reserva
Guayama
Patillas
Arroyo
Aguirre
Point Tuna Lighthouse
Playa Salinas
Playa Santa Isabel

Laguna San Jose

0   5   10   15 miles
0 5 10 15 20Km

N
W — E
S

San Juan, Cruise Ship Docks

the island's dependence on Spanish subsidies (the so-called "situado") and its relative isolation. The island's loyalty was recognized in 1809 when it was declared an overseas province of Spain with the right to send representatives to petition the Spanish court. Royalists from other Spanish colonies also fled to Puerto Rico, and its loyalty was recognized in 1815 after the throne had been restored, by granting Puerto Rico enormous economic freedoms. The island was allowed to trade with non-Spanish countries, and land grants were given to those who had stayed loyal.

The first part of the 19th century saw the development of the plantation economy based on coffee, sugar and tobacco.

For more than 300 years, however, the population consisted largely of Spanish soldiers, merchants and farmers, Taíno Indians, and later African slaves, and there was a lot of inter-racial marrying. When slavery was abolished in 1873, only five percent of the population was pure African, and there were also German, Irish, Scottish, Corsican, Italian and other ethnic communities. By the end of the 19th century, the island's population had almost reached 900,000.

NINETEENTH CENTURY

During the 19th century, the island's trade with the United States increased, and there was a growing resistance to the island's rule by military governors. Calls by island liberals in the 1860s for an end to slavery led to the ringleaders being arrested and sent to Spain for trial. The Aan-Antillian independence movement headed by Cuba led to **El Grito de Lares**, an unsuccessful

rebellion on 23 September 1868. In the same year, however, Queen Isabella II of Spain was forced to abdicate and Spain was declared a Republic, thus all political prisoners were freed, and Puerto Rico was granted a modicum of autonomy. Although this period only lasted from 1868 to 1874, the island's legislature did abolish slavery. After power was restored to the Spanish crown, the autonomist movement grew and in 1897 it was agreed it could form a parliamentary Puerto Rican government, with Spain retaining control over foreign affairs. Before the new parliament could meet, the Spanish-American War broke out in 1898. The war started with the bombing in May of San Juan by US Admiral W.T. Sampson, and the landing of American troops led by General Nelson Miles the following month in the southern town of Guánica. The force met little resistance and an armistice was declared on 12 August.

US ACQUISITION

On 18 December 1898 the island was handed over to the United States and officially ceded to it under the terms of the Treaty of Paris signed on 10 December that year. The island was under a military governor until May 1900 when a US-appointed civilian government was introduced.

At the time of acquisition, the population mostly lived in the countryside, was poor, uneducated, conservative Spanish Catholic by culture and tradition, and resistant to change. The sudden introduction to United States culture, capitalism and commercialism caused social and economic upheavals. Though some administrators, lawyers and such came down, US immigration has been negligible compared to that of Cubans and Dominicans in the last 35 years.

In 1917 under the Jones Act of the US Congress, Puerto Rico became an 'unincorporated territory of the United States' and its people received US citizenship, but there was little provision for local representation in the island's government. The island did prosper, however, although there were huge gulfs between the rich and the poor. Between 1898 and 1939 the acreage under sugar cane increased seven-fold with a ready market in the US. There was massive capital investment in new roads, sugar mills and new strains of disease-resistant crops.

It was not until the 1940s that real economic progress was made, largely due to the efforts of Puerto Rican leader Luis Muñoz Marín, and the US-appointed Governor Rexford Guy Tugwell, who launched 'Operation Bootstrap', to eliminate poverty, and improve education and social conditions. Steps had already been taken to restrict the size of agricultural holdings to 500 acres, so that some land could be returned to small farmers.

Political extremists still argued for Independence and on 1 November 1950, they attempted to assassinate President Truman. There were further acts of violence including an attack in Washington on 1 March 1954, when five congressmen were wounded.

COMMONWEALTH OF PUERTO RICO

In 1952, both the US Congress and the people of Puerto Rico approved a new constitution granting the island limited autonomy. The island was removed from the United Nations' list of non-self-governing jurisdictions and the Common-wealth of Puerto Rico (Estado Libre Asociado de Puerto Rico) was established.

During the 1950's there was large-scale emigration to the United States because of a population explosion on the island and shortage of jobs, and in the 1960s, there was significant immigration from Cuba following Castro's take-over, and also from the Dominican Republic with people looking for work in the fast-developing economy. Despite continued calls for a change in Puerto Rico's status, voters in a 1967 referendum overwhelmingly chose to retain its Commonwealth status. A more recent referendum in 1993 gave a slight advantage to pro-commonwealth autonomists over pro-statehood forces, with independence garnering a small percentage of the vote.

Today, Puerto Rico is relatively prosperous, but there are still political divisions with powerful opposing minority camps who either demand full US statehood, continued autonomic status or complete independence, with the majority supporting continued links with the US in one form or another.

THE PEOPLE

Puerto Rico has a racially mixed population of about 3.9 million, of whom about one million live in and around the San Juan metropolitan area. The people are predominantly Roman Catholic, but religious freedom for all is guaranteed under the Commonwealth Constitution. Puerto Ricans are US citizens and elect a Commissioner to speak for them in the US House of Representatives, but with no voting rights. Islanders do not pay federal taxes and cannot vote for the US president or other federal officials. The island is administered by an elected Governor. Laws are passed by the legislature, consisting of a Senate and House of Representatives and the courts system comprises the third branch of government.

CULTURE

The island's rich culture and heritage reflects its Spanish, African and for the last 100 years or so, its American roots. African influences can be seen in song, dance, music, art and cooking, and there is a determined effort to preserve much of the old Spanish culture, which is reflected in song, dance, costume, cooking and folklore. The Puerto Rican folk-hero is the **jibaro**, the hard working yeoman farmer who toiled to make a living in the hills.

The island has long had a flourishing artistic community working in oils, water colors, ceramics, sculpture, photography and especially the graphic arts, silkscreen prints foremost among them. Several artists have won international acclaim, and their works are increasingly collectible.

The island is particularly noted for the traditional carving of **santos**, small wooden religious figures, often representing a saint. The same families have carved many of these figures for generations with the skills passed down from father to son.

Galleries include Casa Candina, Galeria Bonaire, Galeria Coabey, Galeria Diego and Galeria d'Esopo, among many others, particularly in old San Juan.

Aguas Buenas Artisans

There are fine museums in San Juan and Ponce, excellent theatre and dance groups, and Puerto Rico has produced many fine composers, poets, writers and artists. World-famous cellist **Pablo Casals**, whose mother was Puerto Rican, founded the annual international music festival that still bears his name, after moving to the island in 1957. It is held every June. Puerto Rico also has a fine symphony orchestra, which in 1995 celebrated its 35th season.

National Symbols

National Holiday: November 19
National Song: La Borinquena
National Bird: Striped Tanager (spyndalis zena)
National Flower: Puerto Rican Hibiscus
National Tree: Silk Cotton Tree

LeLo Lai Festival

The Puerto Rico Tourism Company runs a program that allows visitors to experience the history and culture of Puerto Rico at substantial savings. It includes evening performances highlighting the island's Indian, Spanish and African heritage at various San Juan locations from Tuesday to Saturday. It also includes discounted sight-seeing tours, and savings at shops, restaurants and sporting activities throughout the island. Cards can be purchased at tourist offices and participating hotels.

Boqueron Beach

FESTIVALS

Puerto Rico enjoys more festivals and public holidays than most, because it has retained many of the celebrations from its Spanish colonial days, and tagged on all those acquired under US rule. In addition, all towns have their own patron saint and honor them with their own special day or days once a year, with *fiestas patronales*. Festivals are interesting as most are Catholic in origin yet combine Spanish and African customs. Most fiestas take place in the town's central square and some can last up to ten days, with parades and games, music, dancing and lots of eating.

Folklore festivals are also held throughout the island and celebrate events such as the coffee and other crop harvests, and others feature flower exhibitions, musical competitions and local arts and crafts.

The Festival La Casita is a year-round celebration of music and dance, with musicians, dance troupes, orchestras, sculptors, painters and even puppeteers exhibiting their skills every Saturday at La Casita Tourism Information Center, Plaza Dársenas, opposite Pier 1 in Old San Juan. Every Sunday afternoon, there are puppet shows and storytelling at the Children's Theater on the Paseo de la Princesa.

ECONOMY

The standard of living in Puerto Rico is the highest in Latin America and the Caribbean, and in the last forty years enormous strides have been made with the introduction of petrochemical, electronic, high-tech, pharmaceutical, medical equipment and manufacturing industries and development of tourism and its associated service industries. Today, Puerto Rico is the Caribbean's most industrialized island. Most manufacturing industries have to import parts and raw materials, and the rising cost of labor, now approaching US wages, increasingly makes the island less competitive for labor-intensive assembly work. Tourism continues to grow in importance, and rum is also a major export, with 83% of all the rum sold in the US coming from the island.

Traditionally most of the population lived in the mountainous interior and until the mid-1950s, agriculture was the major industry, but there has been a steady migration to the coasts and coastal towns, and the interior population is now small. As the coastal population has increased, many of the towns have merged into large, sprawling urban conurbations close to the manufacturing jobs.

The agriculture sector is now small, producing sugarcane for the rum industry, coffee, tobacco, citrus, pineapple and other tropical fruits. There is some commercial fishing fleet, but the Ponce tuna processing plant relies heavily on catches caught off the African coast. Local tropical hardwoods and bamboo provide materials for the island's small furniture industry.

WEATHER

Puerto Rico enjoys a pleasant year-round climate, although temperatures and rainfall vary depending on altitude. The average annual temperature is 78°F (25°C) with an annual average rainfall of 77 inches (183cm).

The average year-round lowland temperature is 82°F (28°C), and it averages in the mid-80s between November and May. The annual average humidity of 66 % generally makes it feel a few degrees warmer than it actually is, and totally sunless days are rare. There are only a few degrees variation between months with the highest and lowest temperatures. The hottest lowland temperature recorded was 98°F (36°C), and the lowest was 60°F (14°C). Average temperatures in the mountains are on average about 10°F cooler than on the coast during the summer, and up to 20°F cooler in the winter, sometimes down to 40°f at night in the western mountains.

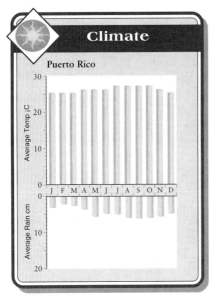

Climate
Puerto Rico

The northeast trade winds bring much of the island's rain, which falls mostly on the north-facing mountain slopes, with much of the south in a rain shadow. The winds also help blow the clouds away, and while it can rain anywhere, it usually doesn't stay wet for long. San Juan on the north coast receives about 60 inches (152cm) of rain a year, El Yunque Peak to the east receives about 180 inches (457cm), while Ponce on the south coast, gets on average only 36 inches (91cm) a year. It rains a bit every month, with the greatest rain falling between May and December.

Hurricanes start as areas of low pressure and grow from a tropical wave to tropical depression and then a tropical storm. When wind speeds top 75mph (120kph), the storm is upgraded to a hurricane. The main hurricane season is from June to November, with August and September generally posing the greatest risk. Because of constant tracking, however, considerable warning is given of the approach of any tropical storm. If a warning is given, follow advice given locally.

PLANT AND ANIMAL LIFE

The lush vegetation and animal life are part of the island's great charm. The island's terrain ranges from beautiful palm-lined beaches along all four coastlines to rugged, mountain ranges, gently rolling hills and dry desert-like areas. There are 20 designated forest reserves, and six more are scheduled. There are also two phosphorescent bays, one off the southwest coast and one off the island of Vieques.

Rainforests

The dense tropical rainforests on the north side of the island are full of massive trees, many more than a 100ft high, and these are draped with vines. Along the branches you can see rare orchids, ferns and huge air plants. **The Caribbean National Forest**, inland from San Juan, contains many rare species of plant, and includes the 28,000-acre (11,200 hectare) **El Yunque Rainforest**, near San Juan - the only tropical rainforest under US Forest Service jurisdiction. There is also **The Guajataca National Forest** with 25 miles (40km) of trails through karst limestone reserves, and **The Guánica Forest Reserve**, a dry forest with the largest number of bird species on the island.

La Coca Falls — El Yunque Rain Forest

The rainforests provide the most prolific vegetation with gumbo-limbo (Bursera simarouba, almácigo in Spanish), and occasional jumbie bead trees with their fascinating black and red seeds, much used for necklaces. There are magnificent swathes of giant tree ferns, towering bamboo groves, enormous air plants, and a host of flowering or variegated plants such as heliconia, philodendron and occasional wild fuchsia in the mountains. There are some trees closely related to balsa, the world's lightest wood, flowering vines and the prolific mountain cabbage palm, and among the foliage and flowers you can find hummingbirds and parrots.

There are palms of all descriptions, giant ferns and bamboos, bananas, coconut groves, breadfruit, breadnut and mango. Some nutmeg and cocoa are planted in a Government-run experimental station in Mayagüez. There is papaya (a name which comes from the Carib word 'ababai', 'fruit of the angels'), and pawpaw, a native North American fruit, Asimina triloba; and the most stunning array of spectacularly colored flowering plants, from giant African tulip trees festooned with scarlet blossoms, to tiny orchids. Bougainvilleas are everywhere, there are scores of varieties of hibiscus, frangipani, plumeria and poinsettias. There are heliconias, also known as lobster plants, bird of paradise flowers and anthuriums everywhere. The flamboyant, also known as the royal poincianna, bursts into bloom during the summer and is a blaze of color.

Because of the lower rainfall, the vegetation in the southern half of the island tends to be mostly thorn, cactus, yucca, mesquite and scrub woodland.

Along the coast you can find swamps, mangroves and marsh woodlands, while inland there are breathtaking walks through tropical rainforests.

Beach morning glory with its array of pink flowers is found on many beaches, and is important because its roots help prevent sand drift. The plant also produces nectar from glands in the base of its leaf stalks that attract ants, and it is thought this evolution has occurred so that the ants will discourage any leaf-nibbling predators. Other beach plants include seagrape and the manchineel, which should be treated with caution.

MANCHINEEL

Note: Although a major eradication campaign has been conducted since the 18th century, the manchineel may be found on some beaches and should be treated with caution. It has a number of effective defensive mechanisms that can prove very painful. Trees vary from a few feet to more than 30 feet in height, and have widely spreading, deep forked boughs with small, dark green leaves and yellow stems, and fruit like small, green apples. If you examine the leaves carefully without touching them, you will notice a small pinhead sized raised dot at the junction of leaf and leaf stalk. The apple-like fruit is very poisonous, and sap from the tree causes very painful blisters. It is so toxic, that early Caribs are said to have dipped their arrowheads in it before hunting trips. Sap is released if a leaf or branch is broken, and more so after rain. Avoid contact with the tree, don't sit under it, or on a fallen branch, and do not eat the fruit. If you do get sap on your skin, run into the sea and wash it off as quickly as possible.

MARINE LIFE

Of course, the sea teems with brilliantly colored fish and often, even more spectacularly colored coral and marine plants. Even if you just float face down in the water with a mask on, you will be able to enjoy many of the beautiful underwater scenes, but the best way to see things is by scuba diving, snorkeling or taking a trip in one of the many glass-bottomed boats.

There are scores of different multi-colored corals that make up the reefs offshore. There are hard and soft corals but only one, the fire coral poses a threat to swimmers and divers, because if touched, it causes a stinging skin rash. Among the more spectacular corals are deadman's fingers, staghorn, brain coral and seafan. There are huge sea anemones and sponges, while tropical fish species include the parrotfish, blue tang surgeonfish, tiny but aggressive damselfish, angelfish and brightly colored wrasse.

COASTAL SWAMPS

Coastal swamps also provide a rich habitat for wildlife. Tiny tree crabs and burrowing edible land crabs scurry around in the mud trapped in the roots of mangrove trees just above water level. Herons, egrets, pelicans and even frigatebirds roost in the higher branches while the mangrove cuckoo shares the lower branches with belted kingfishers.

Gardens are often a blaze of color with flowers in bloom year round, growing alongside exotic vegetables like yam, sweet potato, and dasheen or taro. Flowering plants include the flamboyant tree with their brilliant red flowers which burst into bloom in early summer, and long dark brown seed pods, up to two feet which can be used as rattles when the seeds have dried out inside. Bougainvillea grows everywhere and seems to be in bloom year round in a host of different colors, In fact, the color does not come from petals but the plants' bract-like leaves which surround the small petal-less flowers.

There are yellow, purple and light brown allamandas, poinsettias, hibiscus, anthuriums and multi-colored flowers of the ixora or Maltese cross, as it's called in Puerto Rico.

The leaves of the travelers palm spread out like a giant open fan, and the tree got its name because the thick leaves store water and will yield a drinkable liquid if slashed with a machete.

The flowers attract hummingbirds like the doctorbird, as well as the Carib grackle, a strutting, starling-like bird with a paddle-shaped tail, and friendly bananaquit. You can also spot tree lizards, and the larger geckos that hunt at night.

Along roadsides and hedgerows in the countryside, you can see the vinelike caralito, calabash with its gourd-like fruits, tamarind and distinctive star-shaped leaves of the castor bean, whose seeds when crushed yield castor oil.

Areas of scrubland have their own flora or fauna, with plants bursting into color following the first heavy rains after the dry season. There are century plants, with their prickly, sword-like leaves, which grow for up to twenty years before flowering. The yellow flower stalk grows at a tremendous rate for several days and can reach 20 feet high, but having bloomed once the whole plant then dies. Other typical scrubland vegetation includes aloe, acacia, prickly pear and several species of cactus. Fiddlewood provides hard timber for furniture, highly colored variegated crotons, the white-flowered, aromatic frangipani and sea island cotton, which used to provide the very finest cotton. Scrub vegetation also plays host to birds such as the mockingbird, ground dove, kingbird and grassquit, and it is the ideal habitat for lizards.

On the steep upper slopes is montane vegetation. Many of the trees have aerial roots and are covered in mosses and lichens, native orchids and air plants, and there is usually more ground vegetation because of greater sunlight penetration through the canopy.

The highest altitudes are covered by elfin woodlands, palms, mosses, lichens and ferns. The trees are stunted because there is almost constant wind.

Apart from birds, animal life on the island is not diverse and there are no large animals. There are frogs and toads that croak loudly all night, including the tiny coquí (koh-KEE) frog, which has become the national symbol of Puerto Rico. The frog, which rarely grows to more than one inch (2.5cm) long is very elusive, and gets its name from the cricket-like noise it makes - koh-kee, koh-kee.

There are several species of lizards and non-poisonous snakes, and mongoose that were introduced via Jamaica to eliminate rats that destroyed the crops. Also, there are scores of different insects, including mosquitoes and midges, several species of butterflies, many of them huge, and several species of moth.

Lumbering sea turtles also come ashore at night between March and August to lay their eggs in the sand. Both the rivers and seas teem with fish.

BIRDLIFE

There is a hugely rich bird life with more than 160 species, either resident or visitors on migration. There is one native species of green parrot. There are also bananaquits, mangrove cuckoos, tanagers, ibis, mockingbirds, herons, egrets and many others, including hummingbirds.

Offshore you may see the magnificent frigatebirds, easily recognizable by their size, long black seven-foot wingspan, forked tail and apparent effortless ability to glide on the winds. There are brown booby birds, named by sailors from the Spanish word for 'fool' because they were so easy to catch. Pelicans that look so ungainly on land, yet are so acrobatic in the air, are common, as are laughing gulls and royal terns. Several species of sandpiper can usually be seen scurrying around at the water's edge.

If you are really interested in bird watching, pack a small pair of binoculars. The new mini-binoculars are ideal for island bird watching, because the light is normally so good that you will get a clear image despite the small object lens.

Note: It is an offence to debark any trees, and plants and flowers should not be picked in parks or forest reserves.

As most of the plants, fruits, vegetables and spices will be new to the first-time visitor, the following brief descriptions are offered. Not all these are grown on the island, but all can be found in the markets or could be served to you.

FRUITS

Bananas (guineos in Puerto Rican Spanish) are one of the Caribbean's most important exports, thus their nickname 'green gold' - and they grow everywhere. There are four types of banana commonly available in Puerto Rico; the bananas that we normally buy in supermarkets originated in Malaysia and were introduced into the Caribbean in the early 16th century by the Spanish. A second variety is the red banana, which is not grown commercially, but which can be seen around the island. a third and fourth types are the sweet niño (child) finger-size bananas and the manzano (apple) bananas, velvet-skinned with very delicate taste.

The large "bananas", or plantains (plátanos), a separate species, originally came from Southeast Asia (origin undetermined as yet), and are largely used in cooking. They are often fried, either green and ripe, and served as an accompaniment to fish and meat.

Most banana plantations cover only a few acres and are worked by the owner or tenant, although there are still some very large holdings. A banana produces a crop about every nine months, and each cluster of flowers grows into a hand of bananas. A bunch can contain up to twenty hands of bananas, with each hand having up to 20 individual fruit.

Although they grow tall, bananas are not trees but herbaceous plants which die back each year or so (some varieties take more time to mature). Once the plant has produced fruit, a shoot from the ground is cultivated to take its place, and the old plant dies. Bananas need a lot of attention, and island farmers will tell you that there are not enough hours in a day to do everything that needs to be done. The crop needs fertilizing regularly, leaves need cutting back, and you will often see the fruit inside blue tinted plastic containers, which protect it from insect and bird attack, and speed up maturation.

Captain Bligh

Captain Bligh introduced Breadfruit (pana) to the Caribbean in 1793. He brought 1,200 bread-fruit saplings from Tahiti aboard the Providence, and these were first planted in Jamaica and St. Vincent, and then quickly spread throughout the islands. It was Bligh's attempts to bring in young breadfruit trees that led to the mutiny on the Bounty four years earlier. Bligh was given the command of the 215-ton Bounty in 1787 and was ordered to take the breadfruit trees from Tahiti to the West Indies where they were to be used to provide cheap food for the slaves. The ship had collected its cargo and had reached Tonga when the crew under Fletcher Christian mutinied. The crew claimed that Bligh's regime was too tyrannical, and he and 18 members of the crew who stayed loyal to him, were cast adrift in an open boat. The cargo of breadfruit was dumped overboard. Bligh, in a remarkable feat of seamanship, navigated the boat for 3,600 miles until making landfall on Timor in the East Indies. Some authorities have claimed that it was the breadfruit tree cargo that sparked the mutiny, as each morning the hundreds of trees in their heavy containers had to be carried on deck, and then carried down into the hold at nightfall. It might have proved just too much for the already overworked crew, which had to share their rationed water supply with the plants.

Whatever the reason for the mutiny, the breadfruit is a cheap carbohydrate-rich food, although pretty tasteless when boiled. It is best eaten fried, baked or roasted over charcoal. The slaves did not like them at first, but the tree spread and can now be found almost everywhere. It has large dark, green leaves, and the large green fruits weighing up to 5lbs. The falling fruits explode with a loud "splat" and splatter their pulpy contents over a large distance. It is said that no one goes hungry when the breadfruit is in season. Calabash trees are native to the Caribbean and have huge, inedible gourd-like fruits that are very versatile when dried and cleaned. They can be used as water containers and bowls, bailers for boats, and as lanterns. Juice from the pulp was boiled into a syrup and used to treat coughs and colds, and the fruit is said to have many other medicinal uses.

COCONUT

Coconut palms are everywhere and should be treated with caution. Anyone who has heard the whoosh of a descending coconut and leapt to safety knows how scary the sound is. Those who did not hear the "whoosh" presumably did not live to tell the tale! Actually very few people are injured by falling coconuts and that is a near miracle in view of the tens of thousands of palms all over the island, but it is not a good idea to picnic in a coconut grove!

Coconut trees are incredibly hardy, able to grow in sand even when regularly washed by salty seawater. They can also survive long periods without rain. Their huge leaves, up to 20 feet long in mature trees, drop down during dry spells so a smaller surface area is exposed to the sun which reduces evaporation. Coconut palms can grow up to 80 feet tall, and produce up to 100 seeds a year. The seeds are the second largest in the plant kingdom, and these fall when ripe.

The coconut traditionally bought in greengrocers, is the seed with its layer of coconut surrounded by a hard shell. This shell is surrounded by copra, a fibrous material all contained in a green or yellow husk. A large whole coconut can weigh 5 lbs. or more. The seed and casing are waterproof, drought proof and able to float. In the case of Puerto Rico, it is documented that Spaniards brought them from the Canary Islands before 1550, although there were many edible-fruited palms in America before Columbus (Bactris, Parajubaea, Jessenia, Orbygnia, Acrocomia, etc.), but not coconuts.

The coconut palm is extremely versatile. The leaves can be used as thatch for roofing, or cut into strips and woven into mat and baskets, while the husks yield coir, a fiber resistant to salt water and ideal for ropes and brushes and brooms. Green coconuts contain delicious thirst-quenching 'milk', and the coconut 'meat' can be eaten raw, or baked in ovens for two days before being sent to processing plants where the oil is extracted. Coconut oil is used in cooking, soaps, synthetic rubber and even in hydraulic brake fluid.

Dasheen or taro, is one of the crops known as 'ground provisions' in the Caribbean, the others being sweet potatoes, taniers, manioc and yams. Dasheen with its 'elephant ear' leaves, and eddo grow from a corm which when boiled thoroughly can be used like potato, and the young leaves of either can be used to make calaloo, a spinach-like soup. Tanier is native to the Caribbean, and its roots can be boiled, baked or fried.

Guava is common throughout the West Indies, and the aromatic, pulpy fruit is also a favorite with birds who then distribute its seeds. The fruit-bearing shrub can be seen on roadsides and in gardens, and its fruits are used to make a wide range of products from jelly to 'cheese', a paste made by mixing the fruit with sugar. The fruit, which ranges from a golf ball to a tennis ball in size, is a rich source of vitamin A and contains lots more vitamin C than citrus fruit.

Mango can be delicious if somewhat messy to eat. It originally came from India but is now grown throughout the Caribbean and found wherever there are people. Wild mangoes can be stringy and unappetizing, but ripe fruit from mature trees that grow up to 50 feet and more, are usually delicious, and can be eaten raw or cooked. The juice is a great reviver in the morning, and the fruit is often used to make jams and other preserves.

Passionfruit (parcha) is widely grown and can usually be bought at the market. The pulpy fruit contains hundreds of tiny seeds surrounded by juice sacs, and many people prefer to buy the processed juice or concentrate. It is also commonly used in fruit salads, sherbets and ice creams.

Papaya trees are also found throughout the island and are commonly grown in gardens. The trees are prolific fruit producers but grow so quickly that the fruit soon becomes difficult to gather. The large, juicy melon-like fruits are eaten fresh, pulped for juice or used locally to make jams, preserves and ice cream. They are rich sources of vitamin A and C. The leaves and fruit contain an enzyme which tenderizes meat, and tough joints cooked wrapped in papaya leaves or covered in slices of fruit, usually taste like much more expensive cuts. The same enzyme, papain, is also used in chewing gum, cosmetics, the tanning industry and, somehow, in making wool shrink resistant. A tea made from unripe fruit is said to be good for lowering high blood pressure, as has been medically proven for passion fruit juice.

Pigeon Peas, gandules, are widely cultivated and can be found in many back gardens. The plants are very hardy and drought resistant, and are prolific yields of peas that can be eaten fresh or dried and used in soups and stews.

Pineapples were certainly grown in the Caribbean by the time Columbus arrived, and were brought from South America by the Amerindians. Local fruit is slightly smaller than the Pacific pineapple, but the flavor more intense.

Sugar Cane is still grown commercially but is less important than it was. Most of the cane is grown to produce molasses for the rum industry. The canes can grow up to 12 feet tall, and after cutting, are crushed to extract the sugary juice. After extraction, the juice is boiled until the sugar crystallizes. The mixture remaining is molasses and this is fermented to produce rum.

Sugar apple or anón is a member of the annona fruit family, and grows wild and in gardens throughout the islands. The small, soft sugar apple fruit can be peeled off in strips when ripe, and is like eating thick applesauce. It is eaten fresh or used to make sherbet or drinks. Soursop or guanábana is a member of the same family, and its spiny fruits can be seen in hedgerows and gardens. They are eaten fresh or used for preserves, drinks and ice cream.

Some seasonal tropical fruits you may also encounter are the acerola, a small red berry with the highest vitamin c content of any known fruit; the quenepa, or Spanish lime, a small, green fruit with a sweet/sour flesh surrounding a large seed; the níspero, or sapodilla, a cloyingly sweet morsel with a cinnamon pear taste; the mamey or mammee apple, a huge (up to 10 in/25cm across) fruit with brown skin, orange flesh and apricot-like taste; the avocado, eaten as a vegetable; and many other lesser denizens like the pomarrosa (roseapple), corazón (bullock's heart) and the jagua (genip).

FOOD AND DRINK

Puerto Rico offers a huge choice when it comes to eating out, from excellent traditional island fare to the finest international cuisines. Some of the best local cuisine is found in restaurants displaying the **Mesones Gastronómicos (MG)** symbol, although there are plenty of other good restaurants that are not in the program offering both local and international menus.)

Puerto Rican cuisine is a flavorful blend of Spanish, African and Taíno Indian cooking. Each of these influences has made important contributions to the island's fare in terms of seasoning, cooking methods and basic ingredients.

Cocina criolla, or Creole cuisine, began with the Taínos, the first island settlers. They cultivated many crops, especially yuca - not the plant known in English as yucca - corn, yams and yautía (tanier). Yuca was used to prepare casabe, a flat cassava bread that was eaten daily and is still made and enjoyed today. The Taínos also used yuca to make vinegar, which was an important seasoning and preservative, as they did not use salt in cooking.

Foods introduced by the Spanish include beef, chicken, goat, chickpeas, rice, cilantro, codfish, onions, coconut, garlic and rum. The African slave trade also brought imported foods and techniques to the island, including pigeon peas, sweet potatoes, plantains, okra and cocoyams. The Africans also introduced many dishes using coconut that are still popular today. Their favorite technique was frying, which quickly became the most common method of cooking on the island.

The blending of flavors of ingredients evolved from generation to generation, the marriage of Taíno, Spanish, African and now American, has led to this very exciting 'Comida Criolla' cuisine.

The secret to its success is in the preparation of the ingredients, particularly their spicing or marinades. Island cooks have the added advantage that they have access at almost all times to the freshest ingredients, and they are experts at the subtle blending of herbs and spices.

Dining out in the Caribbean offers the chance to experiment with all sorts of unusual spices, salsas, vegetables and fruits, with Creole and island dishes, and, of course, rum punches and other exotic cocktails.

Eating out is generally very relaxed, and few restaurants have a strict dress code, although most people like to wear something a little smarter at dinner after a day on the beach or out sightseeing. Many hotels have a tendency to offer buffet dinners or barbecues, but even these can be interesting and tasty affairs.

BREAKFAST

Breakfast can be one of the most exciting meals of the day for a visitor. There is a huge range of fruit juices to choose from. Try a glass of watermelon juice, followed by a fresh grapefruit, or slices of chilled papaya or mango. Most hotels offer fruit plates offering a wide choice so you should be able to taste your way through them all during your stay.

The island's fruits also make great jams and preserves, and you can follow the fruit with piping hot toast spread with perhaps citrus marmalade or guava jam, perhaps washed down with the island's own coffee. Most hotels also offer traditional gargantuan American breakfasts for those who can't do without them.

LUNCH

Lunches are best eaten at beach cafes and grills, which usually offer excellent barbecued fresh fish and conch. Lobster and crab are also widely available. Dishes are often served with rice and local vegetables such as fried plantain, cassava and yam, and fresh fruit such as pineapple, mango or papaya makes an ideal and light dessert. There is a steady supply of fruit through the year as different varieties have different seasons. During the summer, there are fruits such as the quenepa, roseapple (pomarrosa), sugar apple and ambarella, a mango relative. Also used is Spanish lime or quenette; while golden apple (jobo de la india) may be offered but is uncommon.

Green bananas and plantains are usually eaten raw, or boiled or steamed in the skin, then cut into slices and served very hot. They also make excellent chips when fried, called tostones.

If traveling around, there are fast food stalls that offer tasty snacks, usually fried. The favorite foods from fritter stands are bacalaitos, alcapurrias, pastelillos and empanadillas and piononos. Fried pork chops and tostones are also usually available.

DINNER

There is an enormous choice when it comes to dinner. A great way to sample the real Puerto Rican cuisine is to eat in restaurants in the Mesones Gastronómicos program. These establishments are chosen because they offer both the highest standards and specialize in local cuisine.

Starters include a huge choice of locally grown and produced fruit juices from orange and grapefruit to the more unusual ones like soursop and tamarind. You can also drink green coconut 'milk'.

You can find alcapurrias, made from grated yautía (tanier) and stuffed with meat, crab or lobster, green bananas stuffed with picadillo, which is cooked ground meat (mince meat), crabmeat or chicken. Piononos, rolled, ripe plantain strips filled with meat. Empanadillas and pastelillos are small, deep-fried flour turnovers filled with cheddar or swiss cheese, ground meat or shredded chicken. Bacalaitos are flour fritters made from salt codfish, surrullos de maíz or surrullitos, are made of cornmeal, shaped like a cigar and served with a sauce made from ketchup and mayonnaise, and rellenos de papa, mashed potato balls stuffed with almost any filling, and deep fried.

The national soup of Puerto Rico is asopao, a hearty chicken and rice-like gumbo, which is so filling it can serve as a main course too. It can also be made with lobster or shrimp. It takes time to prepare in a restaurant but the wait is worth it. Most traditional soups, somewhere between soups and stews, are based on a combination of assorted root vegetables, meats and a sofrito-based sauce.

Traditional Caribbean starters also include dishes such as Christophene and coconut soup, and Callaloo soup made from the young leaves of dasheen, a spinach-like vegetable. The soup is made throughout the Caribbean and okra, smoked meat and sometimes crab are added, as well as lots of herbs and spices. Chicken nuggets and marinated green bananas (guineito en escabeche) are also popular appetisers.

Fish and clam chowders are also popular starters. Try heart of palm, excellent fresh shrimps or scallops, smoked kingfish wrapped in crepes or crab backs, succulent land crab meat sautéed with breadcrumbs and seasoning, and served in the shell. It is much sweeter than the meat of sea crabs.

SEA FOOD

The fish is generally excellent, and don't be alarmed if you see dolphin on the menu. It is not the protected species made famous by 'Flipper', but a solid, close-textured flat-faced fish called the dorado, which is delicious. Many of the fish dishes are based on Spanish cuisine, and are often prepared in a sofrito-based sauce or escabeche style, a marinade of olive oil, white vinegar and spices.

Bacalao is salt cod (codfish), which was a staple food on the island for centuries. Salting was the most common form of food preserving, and allowed surplus catches to be safely kept until times of food shortage, or for when the seas were too rough for the fishing boats to go to sea.

There is also snapper, grouper, kingfish, redfish, jacks, balaouy, snapper, tuna, flying fish, lobster, swordfish, baby squid and mussels. There are delicious river crayfish and langostinos that are the larger saltwater variety, mussels and oyster.

Try seafood asopao, chunks of lobster, shrimps and ham served on a bed of braised seasoned rice, shrimp Creole, with fresh shrimp sautéed in garlic butter and parsley and served with tomatoes, or fish Creole, with fresh fish steaks cooked in a spicy onion, garlic and tomato sauce and served with rice and fried plantain. Other island dishes may include sautéed scallops with ginger, curried fish steaks lightly fried with a curry sauce and served with sliced bananas, cucumber, fresh coconut and rice.

PUERTO RICAN CUISINE

It seems such a waste to travel to the Caribbean and eat burgers and steaks, especially when there are many much more exciting meat dishes available.

Many of the favorite Puerto Rican main meat dishes are rich in beef or pork. Roast suckling pig, a national dish, has traditionally been served on festive occasions and holidays, and is delicious. Steak and onions is an everyday dish, as are stuffed pot roast and pork ribs stewed or prepared with yellow rice and green pigeon peas. **Lechon asado** (roast suckling pig) is the national dish and magnificent.

Chicken is also served in countless ways, and eaten almost daily. Chicken and turkey may be seasoned with adobo, a dry marinade made from salt, crushed peppercorns, Puerto Rican oregano (lippium graveolens), garlic salt, and sometimes cumin, which is rubbed over the meat. **Arroz con pollo** is another island specialty – chicken rubbed with adobo and then cooked in onions, peppers, garlic, rice and often beer.

You may find a restaurant offering Leeward and Windward Island fare such as curried chicken served in a coconut shell, oven baked chicken with pineapple and mango, curried goat served with freshly grated coconut, gingered chicken with mango and spices. There is also tripe and black (blood) pudding.

Puerto Rican cuisine also offers traditional side dishes, such as **arroz blanco**, which is white rice boiled in water and oil, habichuelas, beans stewed in sofrito, a puree of onions, peppers, recao (a native herb, eryngium foetidum) cilantro, garlic and salt pork, and a tomato and coriander sauce which are widely served with main courses. **Tostones** are twice-fried green plantains, and delicious.

Mofongo is another popular side dish, and consists of fried green plantains mashed with garlic, salt and fried pork rinds and rolled into a ball. Mofongo can be served with caldo (beef or chicken broth), or carne frita, which is diced and fried pork. Amarillos is another favorite, thin, long slices of ripe yellow plantain sautéed in butter or olive oil, or more often, fried.

For vegetarians there are excellent salads, stuffed breadfruit, callaloo bake, stuffed squash, eggplant or papaya, baked sweet potato and yam casserole.

For dessert, try postre (fresh fruit salad) with added cherry juice, and sometimes a little rum, which is a year round popular dessert. The national dish is flan, a condensed milk and vanilla custard, which can be filled with cream cheese, coconut milk, mashed pumpkin or bread-fruit. Puerto Rico has a traditional bread pudding, and also offers tembleque, a gelatin-like coconut milk and cornstarch custard often eaten sprinkled with cinnamon. Arroz con dulce is rice pudding cooked with condensed coconut milk, ginger and raisins, and there are a wide variety of fruit sherbets using tropical fruits such as soursop and tamarind.

Or, try one of the exotically flavored ice creams. There are also banana fritters and banana flambé, coconut cheesecake, green papaya or guava shells simmered in heavy syrup and served with white or cottage cheese.

Most menus and dishes are self-explanatory, with dishes given in Spanish and English. Bananas are called guineos, and plantains, plátanos, whereas in the rest of the Spanish-speaking world bananas are plátanos and plantains are plátanos machos. The first bananas in Puerto Rico came from Africa and thus were called plátanos de Guinea, later shortened to guineos.

Salt fish was traditionally salted cod, but now it can be any fish.

There are wonderful breads in the Caribbean, and you should try them if you get the chance. There are banana and pumpkin breads, and delicious cakes such as coconut loaf cake, guava jelly cookies and rum cake.

Don't be afraid to eat out. Food is often prepared in front of you, and there are some great snacks available from island eateries, especially fritters and pit-roasted pork. **Lechonera stalls** specialize in 'fast food' pork dishes.

A note of warning: on most tables you will find a bottle of pepper sauce, called **pique** (pee-keh). It usually contains a blend of several types of hot pepper, spices and vinegar, and should be treated cautiously. Try a little first before splashing it all over your food, as these sauces range from hot to unbearable.

If you want to make your own hot pepper sauce, take four ripe hot peppers (ajíes picantes), one teaspoon each of oil, ketchup and vinegar and a pinch of salt, blend together into a liquid, and bottle.

DRINKS

Rum is the Caribbean drink, and Puerto Rico is home to Bacardi, the world's largest distillery. There are free guided tours Monday to Saturday from 8.30am to 4.30pm. ☎ 788-8400.

There are almost as many rums in the West Indies as there are malt whiskies in Scotland, and there is an amazing variety of strength, color and quality. Other famous brand names include Don Q and Barrilito. The finest rums are best drunk on the rocks, but if you want to capture a bit of the Caribbean spirit, have a couple of rum punches.

RUM PUNCH

To make Plantation Rum Punch, thoroughly mix three ounces of rum, with one ounce of limejuice and one teaspoon of honey, then pour over crushed ice, and for a little zest, add a pinch of freshly grated nutmeg.

Most hotels and bars also offer a wide range of cocktails both alcoholic, usually very strong, and non-alcoholic. Beer, drunk cold and from the bottle, is the most popular drink, and Puerto Rico has several good beers, especially Medalla, and a good selection of imported wines. Puerto Rico is also famous for Piña Colada, a cocktail of rum, pineapple juice and cream of coconut, which was created on the island.

An excellent way to finish a meal is with a cup of aromatic Puerto Rican coffee, either black or with frothy boiled milk.

Tap water is safe to drink as are ice cubes made from it. Mineral and bottled water is widely available, and so are soft drinks.

Note: While many of the restaurants do offer excellent service, time does not always have the same urgency as it does back home, and why should it after all, as you are on holiday. Relax, enjoy a drink, the company and the surroundings and don't worry if things take just a little longer, the wait is generally worth it.

Island Tours

group which will make it even better value. Apart from a trip to San Juan, which is a must, there are the forest reserves to explore, the Spanish colonial towns, the mountains, the many secluded beaches and off-shore world-class diving. There are spectacular forest walks and nature trails, and a wealth of land and water sports as well as massive caves to explore. As you travel around the island you will find a wide range of restaurants from beach grills to the charming and picturesque country inns - **Paradores Puertorriqueños**, of which there are now 24. The problem is not deciding what to do, but finding time to do it all.

BY ROAD

Taxis, buses and rental cars are available at the airport and major hotels.

Taxis labeled **taxi turístico**, are readily available (especially outside hotels and tourist attractions), and charge fixed rates for certain standard tourist routes, which are prominently labeled in each taxi and at the airport. These are:

From the international airport to: Isla Verde $8, Condado $12, Old San Juan $16. Rates from piers to: Old San Juan $6, Puerta de Tierra $6, Condado $10, and Isla Verde $16. For other routes, they and other taxis not labeled taxi

GETTING AROUND

The island is large by Caribbean standards and a rental car is the best way of getting around if you want to do a lot of exploring. The main roads are generally very good and allow you to cover a lot of ground quickly if you need to.

If you simply want to laze on the beach near your hotel and only spend a couple of days sightseeing, take one of the many organized tours or hire a taxi for the day, especially if you can make up a turístico may also be hired by the meter, which they all have, at an initial charge of $1, and the meter then increases for every one third of a mile traveled or 45 seconds spent as waiting time. There is an additional charge of 50¢ for large pieces of luggage carried and $1 for trunks (fixed rate routes allow two pieces of luggage at no extra charge). There is a night surcharge for trips between 10pm and 6am.

Taxis can also be rented by the hour for about $20, for longer trips and half and full day sightseeing tours. Make sure you agree on the price before setting off.

The public bus service – AMA – operates in the greater San Juan area linking the main business, shopping and tourist areas. Routes A5 and B21 will get you to and from most of the tourist areas. Bus stops are marked '**Parada**' and the buses display the number of route they are on. The fee is 25c or 50c depending on how far you are traveling and you must have the exact fare. The last buses run around 9pm – earlier on Sundays.

Públicos are 'public cars' or mini-vans, which run at regular intervals on fixed routes to towns throughout the island. They usually operate during daylight hours, leave from the main square or special designated areas and have fixed fares. as long as there's room you may ride, but you may have to wait for the vehicle to fill before it will leave.

Cangrejos Yacht Club, San Juan Metro, Marinas

BY BOAT

There are car and passenger ferries to and from Culebra and Vieques from Fajardo. Reservations are required for cars, and it is advisable to ring to check departure times ☎ 863-0705/0852.

The Catano ferry crosses San Juan Harbor from Old San Juan to Cataño and the Bacardí Rum Distillery, where there are free tours. The ferry crossing costs 50¢ and it is worth it, even if you don't plan to visit Bacardí. The ferries run every half hour in each direction between 6am and 9pm, and from Cataño to Bacardí is just a short público or taxi ride. ☎ 788-1155 or 723-2260.

BY AIR

From either the international or regional airports in San Juan, there are daily flights to many cities and towns throughout Puerto Rico. There is also a quick and inexpensive air service from Fajardo to the islands of Culebra and Vieques.

NOTE

When asking for directions, you will often be given the names of the streets of the nearest intersection rather than details of how to get to a specific address.

SAN JUAN

The capital is a huge sprawling city with a population of around one million, one third of the island's people. You need at least two or three days to explore it fully and at leisure. It has beaches and luxury hotels, a vast cosmopolitan shopping area, historic sights and museums, great restaurants and bars, and a vibrant nightlife catering to almost all tastes. The metropolitan area consists of three distinct areas - Old San Juan, the beach and resort area and the outlying suburbs.

The modern town has art galleries and boutiques, top name designer shops and stores, and casinos and concert halls. The seven-acre (three-hectare) block of Old San Juan was rightly declared a **National Historic Zone** in the 1950s and deserves at least a day's exploration. It has museums, churches, forts, a multitude of beautifully restored old buildings, many of them delightful private homes, and a wide range of restaurants, bars and sidewalk cafés. There are also boutiques and galleries. The area contains some of the finest examples of 16th and 17th century Spanish colonial architecture in the Western Hemisphere.

OLD SAN JUAN

Note: A free trolley service operates from the La Puntilla and Covadonga parking areas. The 30-minute ride gives you a good overview of the old city before you set off to explore on foot.

The original city was founded in 1521 and is the oldest capital city under the US flag. Its major landmark is the imposing and impressive **Fuerto San Felipe del Morro**, better known as El Morro. It was built between 1540 and 1586 to protect both the town and its harbor although construction continued on and off until the late 18th century. Morro is Spanish for headland, and the fort reflects the steep terrain on which it was built, and actually has six levels. The battlements stand 140 feet (43m) above the sea, and the walls in places are 18 feet (5m) thick. British privateer **Sir Francis Drake** was one of the many fleet commanders who were unsuccessful in trying to breach its defenses. The fortress was taken only once, in 1538 after a land assault by English troops under the Earl of Cumberland. The force was landed up the coast and launched their surprise attack as the defenders looked out to sea for the enemy's approach. The fort is a marvelous example of the skills of the military engineers, and is a warren of tunnels, dungeons, barracks, outposts and ramps. It was completed in 1771 but work began again in 1783 to strengthen the defences. There is a small but interesting museum that traces the history and development of the fort.

Fort San Cristóbal was built as El Morro's partner in defence of the city. It stands 150 feet (46m) above the sea and covers 27 acres (11 hectares) of land. Apart from its sheer intimidating size, it was designed so that if the outer walls were breached, attackers would have to fight every inch of their way through an elaborate defensive network of inner walls to penetrate the heart of the fort. Also it was designed in such a way, that each area within the fort was a self-contained unit with its own defenses, moat and tunnels, so that if one part fell to the enemy, the others could continue to fight on. The forts are open daily and both have been designated World Heritage and National Historic Sites.

Construction of the massive **La Muralla** (City Wall) that surrounds the old town was started in the 1630s. They consist of two huge parallel walls, 42 feet (13m) high, built out of solid sandstone blocks held together by a limestone and mortar mix. The gap between the two walls was then filled with sand. The exterior facing wall was built so that it sloped for added strength and stability. At its base the City Wall was about 20 feet (6m) thick, sloping to about 12 feet (4m) at the top. **San Gerónimo** was the city's other fort.

The **San Juan Gate** was built in 1520 and is the only one that remains of the six original gates in the City Wall. Every night the huge wooden doors would be closed sealing the city off from attack. Most of the wall was torn down at the turn of the century to allow the old city to grow.

Inside the City Walls, **Old San Juan** covers seven blocks that started as a fortified district, and is now a charming area of museums, private houses and businesses. Six buildings in the old town have been designated world-class historic sites by the United Nations. The ancient streets are cobbled in a blue stone called adoquín that is made from furnace slag, and it was used as ballast on the Spanish merchant ships. The streets are steep and narrow and during the day are packed with motor traffic, so the best way to explore is on foot. It is also worth taking a cruise of the harbor, either on a tour boat or by taking the ferry across to **Cataño**, as this is the only real way of appreciating just how impressive the city's fortifications must have appeared to approaching ships. The tour boats take in the El Morro fortress, and cruise past Casa Blanca, the City Walls, San Juan Gate, La Fortaleza and the Customs House, while the ferry not only gives you a great view of the old town, but also takes you across to the **Bacardí Rum Distillery**, the largest in the world.

Both tour boats and ferries leave from Pier 2.

Old San Juan has many plazas. The **Plaza de San José** is a popular meeting place and is dominated by the statue of Ponce de León, made from a melted down British cannon that was captured in 1797. Adjoining it is **Plaza del Quinto Centenario** that stands at the highest point in Old San Juan and offers fine views over the city and the Atlantic Ocean. It also makes a good starting point for your exploration of the old town. The plaza was built as part of the 1992-3 celebrations to mark the 500th anniversary of the discovery of the **New World**, and is dominated by the 40 foot (12m) black granite and ceramics totem-like sculpture which rises from the top level of the square. The statue symbolizes the earthen and clay roots of Puerto Rican history and was created by **Jaime Suárez**, one of Puerto Rico's foremost artists. From its southern end, two needle-shaped columns point skywards to the North Star, the guiding light of explorers, and around the plaza are fountains, and other columns and sculpted steps that represent various periods in the island's 500-year history. The square is also an ideal place for getting your bearings and an overview of the old town, with views across to El Morro on the headland of San Juan Bay and to the Dominican Convent and **San José Church**, a wonderful example of true Gothic architecture, and a

Castillo San Cristóbal, Old San Juan

OLD SAN JUAN

Castillo del Morro

Calle Del Morro

La Muralla (City Wall)

San Juan Blvd

Norzagaray Blvd

Fuerte San Cristóbal

Plaza de Quincentenia

Plaza San José ⑰ ⑯ ⑱ ⑲

Beneficiencia

San Sebastian

Cruz

San Sol

Tanca

Las Monjas ①

Luna

O'Donell

Plaza de Colón ⑥

Muñoz Rivera

Ponceo de Covadonga

San Juan Gate ★

⑬

⑭ ⑮

San Justo Francisco

San José

⑫

Cristo

San Juan

Plaza de Armas

Fortaleza

⑦

⑤

Paseo

Allen

Las Palomas Park

⑪ ⑩

⑧ ⑨

Tetuan

Recinto Sur

Comercio

④

Paseo

De La Princesa

②

Calle

Marina

③

i

Presidio

Puntillo

P

El Arsenal

N
W ● ● ● E
S

① Casa Blanca
② Main Post Office
③ Museum of the Seas
④ Plazoleta del Puerto
⑤ Tapia Theater
⑥ Casino
⑦ Casa de Callejón
⑧ Crito Chapel
⑨ Bastión de las Palmas
⑩ Casa del Libro
⑪ Fine Arts Museum
⑫ Felisa Rincón de Gautier Museum
⑬ Gran Hotel El Convento
⑭ San Juan Cathedral
⑮ City Hall
⑯ Museum of Art & History
⑰ Pablo Casals Museum
⑱ San José Church
⑲ Casa de los Contrafuentes
⑳ Dominican Convent

| 0 | 100 | 200 | 300 | 400 | 500 m |
| 0 | 100 | 200 | 300 | 400 | 500 yds |

Castillo San Felipe del Morro, Old San Juan

rarity in the New World. You can also look over the **Asilo de Beneficencia**, built in 1832, as a hospital for the poor, which stands on the corner by the entrance to the El Morro fortress, and is now the home of the **Institute of Puerto Rican Culture**, which has done such an excellent job on restoring and preserving the island's heritage.

Next to the Plaza is the **Cuartel de Ballajá**, built in the mid-19th century as the Spanish Army headquarters, and still the largest building in the Americas constructed by Spanish engineers. It was declared a National Historic Monument in 1954 and now houses the **Museum of the Americas** (see below).

Other old town plazas are **Las Palomas** Park, on the top of the city wall overlooking the restored **La Princesa** jail - now the headquarters of the Puerto Rico Tourism Company and a fascinating gallery, open Monday to Friday 9am to 4pm. ☎ 721-2400. There is also **Plaza de Armas**, in front of city hall, **Plaza Colón**, with a statue dedicated to Columbus, a small plaza behind the **Tapia Theater** (722-0407) built in 1832, and the **Plazoleta del Puerto**, alongside the cruise ship dock, which is noted for its arts and crafts. Here craftsmen sell their wares around the patio of a refurbished warehouse. You can buy the wooden figurines known as santos, carved dolls in traditional costumes, guitars, ceramic works, woven baskets, other hand made specialties, and paintings.

The **Paseo de La Princesa** is one of Old San Juan's most attractive boulevards. During the 19th century, it was where the Spanish gentry strolled, and today, after a recent multi-million dollar program, it has been restored to its former glory. The **Paseo** runs from the piers which welcome the hundreds of visiting cruise ships, past **La Princesa**, the former 19th century prison which has been restored and now houses the Puerto Rico Tourism Company, runs round the old city walls beneath **Casa Blanca**, once the home of the Ponce de León family, and continues to the entrance to the 16th century El Morro fortress. The broad esplanade, repaved with new brick, is lined with towering Royal Palms, and on the west side, overlooking the Atlantic Ocean and its balmy breezes, is a large bronze fountain, the work of Spanish artist Luis Sanguino. The sculpture s entitled 'Raíces" (Roots), and it depicts the Indian, African and Spanish origins of Puerto Rico as human figures standing among cavorting dolphins. Along the east side of the Paseo there is a group of five sculptures by José Buscaglia, representing scenes from the island's history and heritage. In front of La Princesa there is a statue of **Doña Felisa Gautier**, one of the island's most popular leaders, and the first woman mayor of San Juan, from 1946 to 1968. A museum dedicated to her life is in **Caleta de San Juan**. It is open Monday to Friday 9am to 4pm. ☎ 723-1897.

The Paseo is still a delightful place to take the sea air and enjoy the views, and you can stop to enjoy the work of artisans or for a snack, light meal or drink along the way. There is a gazebo offering seafood, salads and delicious coffee and you can sit out at tables under the shade of the trees, or you can try some of the tasty 'criollo' dishes from the brightly colored food carts.

It pays to plan your visit to Old San Juan because there is so much to see and do in such a small area that it is easy to overlook many of its treasures. It is best to travel in by taxi, as the only way to explore the city is on foot, and there are always taxis at stands to run you home after your visit. Old San Juan sits on a peninsula about one mile (1.6km) long at its longest and about half a mile (.8km) across at its widest point.

Start at **Castillo del Morro**, or El Morro fort that Stands on the headland at the west of the Old Town. A visit to the fort immediately sets the scene. The fortress itself is magnificent and has changed little over the years. It offers spectacular views over both the sea approaches and the old city. Then stroll down Calle del Morro to its junction with San Sebastián to visit Casa Blanca on your right. Make your way to Caleta De Las Monjas that runs along the south shore with the impressive La Muralla (City Wall), between you and the sea. You pass through the San Juan Gate and the road then becomes the pretty Paseo de la Princesa. The promenade runs past La Princesa and the headquarters of the tourist office on your right, and La Puntilla promontory on your right with El Arsenal. There is public parking here and the free trolley service operates from here as well. Inland is the main Post Office near the corner of Cruz and Fortaleza

The Paseo de la Princesa then connects with Paseo Gilberto Concepcion de Gracia, the street that runs past the cruise ship dock and ferry terminals that receive more than a million visitors annually. On your right is the pink Customs Building and then the La Casita Tourist Information Center. The **Museum of the Seas** is housed on Pier One. Opposite Pier Two is the **Plazoleta del Puerto**, and you then cut inland to Recinto Sur that runs east past the Tapia Theater close to the junction with Fortaleza and its many restaurants, and Ponce de León streets. Across the junction is the magnificent Casino and opposite it is the Plaza Colón. Head west on Fortaleza past the Casa del Callejón on the right, and then turn left into San José to its junction with Tetuán. Opposite is the **Bastión de las Palmas**, and if you then turn right into Cristo Street you have the Cristo Chapel and Las Palomas Park on your left with La Fortaleza beyond, and **Casa del Libro** and then the **Fine Arts Museum** on your right. Retrace your route to Cristo Street again and head north to its junction with San Francisco Street. To the left is the **Felisa Rincón de Gautier Museum** close to the city wall, opposite is the **Gran Hotel El Convento**, and to your right across the junction are the **San Juan Cathedral** and the former Provincial Assembly Building. Head east on San Francisco street past the junction with San José street with Casa San José and **City Hall** on your left and Plaza de Armas on your right. Turn left into Cruz Street, and then right into Sol Street and continue to the end to visit **Fort San Cristóbal** and the San Juan National Historic Site Headquarters. Then follow Norzagaray Boulevard round beneath the city walls to its junction with Mercado Street. Here, bordering Plaza San José are the **Museum of Art and History**, the **Pablo Casals Museum**, **San José Church**, and **Casa de los Contrafuertes.** To the right of Norzagaray Boulevard is the **Dominican Convent**, and this tour ends opposite in the magnificent Plaza del Quinto Centenario.

MUSEUMS OF OLD SAN JUAN

It has been said that there are more museums in Old San Juan than in any other comparable area on earth. In fact, there are many who claim that the whole of the old town is one large living museum because of its history and wealth of old buildings, many of which are National Historic Sites.

The **Archives and General Library** was originally built in 1877 as a hospital and then became a prison. Since then it has been a cigar factory and rum distillery and it now houses the library and archives of the Institute of Puerto Rican Culture.

Casa Blanca – Puerto Rico's 'White House' – was built in 1523 as the family home of Ponce de León, and today houses a fascinating **Taíno Indian Ethno-Historic Museum**, as well as as the **Juan Ponce de León Museum**, with exhibits about the island's first Governor, his family and their lifestyle in the early 16th century. The house on San Sebastian overlooking San Juan Bay, was built on land granted to Ponce de León by Spanish King Charles I as a reward for his exploration and settlement of Puerto Rico. Tragically, Ponce de León never lived in the house. He was killed by a poison-tipped arrow in Florida the year the house was built, and it passed to his family who lived there for 250 years, When it was originally built, its massive walls served as the island's only fortress and on several occasions it sheltered the inhabitants of San Juan from attacks by Carib Indians. It continued to serve as the island's citadel until 1540 when La Fortaleza, now the Governor's residence, was built. The Ponce de León family lived in the house until 1779 when it was sold to the Spanish Government, and from 1898 at the end of the Spanish-American War until 1967, it was the official home of the Commander of the US Army on the island. It is believed to be the oldest continuously occupied residence in the Western Hemisphere, and is also the oldest of the 800 Spanish colonial buildings in Old San Juan. The mansion was declared a National Historic Monument in 1968 and formerly housed a museum of 16th and 17th century family life on the island.

The house has now been restored by the Institute of Puerto Rican Culture and furnished with authentic 16th and 17th century furnishings and fixtures, and the Puerto Rican Tourism Company assisted with the restoration of the beautiful gardens and fountains. Although the building is no longer a home, it houses the two museums dedicated to the Spanish explorer and the Taíno Indians. ☎ 724-5477.

THE TAÍNOS

The **Taíno Indian Ethno-Historic Museum** is on the upper level of the house, and recreates the life and culture of Puerto Rico's first inhabitants. The Taínos were Arawak Amerindians from Venezuela in South America, who had spread throughout the Greater Antilles by the time of Columbus' voyages. They survived, however, for only 100 years or so after the arrival of the Spanish.

When the Spanish first arrived, the Taínos grew cassava and corn as their staple crops, foraged for fruits and berries and hunted for small animals, birds and fish. Settlements

Casa Blanca, Old San Juan

ranged in size from single homes to communities of 2-3,000, and homes were built of pole-supported reed walls with thatched roofs. They wore few if any clothes, but painted themselves on special occasions and wore jewelry such as ear and nose rings and necklaces. Some of this jewelry was made of gold that attracted the Spanish who thought there were rich pickings to be had on Puerto Rico.

When the Taínos greeted the first Spaniards, they told them that gold nuggets could be picked up from the island's rivers, and invited the strangers to help themselves.

Columbus wrote in his diary: 'Gold constitutes treasure and he who possesses it, has all he needs in this world. He has the means of restoring souls to the enjoyment of paradise.'

The Taínos were also accomplished weavers and potters, and carved in stone and wood.

The museum traces their life through ceremonial objects and everyday objects, and you can explore a replica of a Taíno village or 'yucayeque,' and see how they cultivated their crops, hunted, built canoes, and performed their religious ceremonies. Of particular interest are a series of 16th century European maps of the world as it was known then, with reproductions of paintings of Columbus and charts of his voyages. It was on his second voyage that he discovered what the Indians called '**Borikén**' - 'the land of the proud lord.' Also of interest is a display that traces the various indigenous groups still living in Venezuela from which the Taínos came.

The **Juan Ponce de León Museum** is on the ground floor, and traces life in the house from the 16th to 18th centuries with important period furnishings and works of art. Star exhibits include the carved Conquistador's coat of arms just inside the entrance, the three-key chest that was used to hold all the official Crown documents, and the Throne Room intended for use by the Spanish king. There are also displays of military weapons, early scientific experiments by Ponce de León's grandson, and objects of everyday life. The house is open from 9am to noon and 1pm to 4.30pm from Tuesday to Sunday. ☎ 724-4102.

Casa del Callejón is also run by the Institute of Puerto Rican Culture and houses two museums - the Museum of Colonial Architecture, and the Museum of the Puerto Rican Family. Both are open from Wednesday to Sunday.

One of the buildings off the Plaza San José is the Casa de los Contrafuertes, 101 San Sebastian, thought to be the oldest private residence in Old San Juan, and dating from the early 18th century. On the upper floor is the Latin American Graphic Arts Museum and Gallery, while the ground floor features the Pharmacy Museum, an exact replica of a 19th century drugstore with scales and old bottles. The museums are open from 9am to 4.30pm Wednesday to Sunday ☎ 724-5477.

The 18th century Casa del Libro is near the end of Cristo Street, and houses a collection of more than 5,000 rare books, many of them dating back to the 16th century. There are also documents signed by Ferdinand and Isabella of Spain, and exhibits about the history of bookmaking. The library is open from 10am to 4.30pm Tuesday to Saturday ☎ 723-0354.

In the grounds of El Morro is the Cuartel de Ballajá, which used to house the Spanish troops and their families. It has been fully restored and now houses the Museum of the Americas. It features changing exhibitions, archaeological items found in the Ballajá area, and displays of crafts from the Americas. It is open from 10am to 4pm Tuesday to Friday, and from 11am to 5pm on weekends ☎ 724-5052.

The most spectacular museum is the Fuerte San Felipe del Morro, better known as El Morro fort. The sheer size of the fort is breathtaking, and it is the most impressive and dramatic of the city's fortifications. It contains a small museum with maps, models of old shops and exhibits on military life.

Together with Fort San Cristóbal, El Morro is a National Historic Site and part of a World Heritage Site. It is open daily from 9am to 5pm, with conducted tours available, orientation leaflets and video presentations in English and Spanish ☎ 729-6960.

The Felisa Rincón de Gautier Museum honors the first woman to serve as mayor of San Juan, and also offers a fascinating insight into a typical Old San Juan home. The former residence of Doña Felisa is on Caleta de San Juan, and includes photographs and documents high-lighting her colorful career. It also includes her dresses and elaborate wigs, as well as the many awards and honorary degrees presented to her, together with the ceremonial keys to cities throughout North America and Europe. It is open from 9am to 4pm from Monday to Friday ☎ 723-1897.

The **Fine Arts Museum** is housed in the **Institute of Puerto Rican Culture**. The building was originally constructed as a Dominican friary in 1523 and was rebuilt in the 1840s as a poor house, the **Asilo de Beneficencia**. It has two delightful inner patios, and now houses the Institute and several galleries with changing exhibits of paintings and sculptures. It is open from 9am to 4.30pm Wednesday to Saturday ☎ 724-5949.

La Princesa, a former jail and now the headquarters of the Puerto Rico Tourism Company, also houses a gallery of island art which is open from 9am to 4pm Monday to Saturday ☎ 721-2400.

The Museum of the Indian is in **Casa de los Zaguanes**, the house of two halls in San José Street, and tells the story of the island's indigenous people with displays, exhibits, tools and examples of their arts and crafts, including stone pictographs of monkeys and pelicans. It is open daily from 9am to noon and 1pm to 4.30pm ☎ 721-5274.

The **Museo del Niño**, (Children's Museum), is a new museum for both the young and old. Very young children can gain admission by crawling between the legs of a large wooden figure of a child, and inside there is a village of playhouses, and a popular 'visit the dentist' exhibit, in which children can play the role of dentist. It is open from 9.30am to 3.30pm Tuesday to Thursday and from 11am to 4pm at the weekend ☎ 722-3791.

The **Pablo Casals Museum**, on the corner of Cristo and San Sebastián Streets in historic Plaza San José, honors the world famous cellist who spent the last 20 years of his life on the island. His mother was born on Puerto Rico and he returned to his roots to promote music on the island. The museum has a collection of the musician's memorabilia, manuscripts, photographs and videotapes of concerts. It is open from 9.30am to 5pm Tuesday to Saturday ☎ 723-9185. The island's prestigious annual music festival still bears his name.

The Plaza San José is noted for its many historic buildings, and also has a statue of Juan Ponce de León.

The **Museum of the Sea**, housed on the ground floor of the Pier One building at the Cruise Ship terminal, has displays about maritime history and features model ships, old maps, navigational equipment and other nautical instruments. The museum is open whenever the pier is open for cruise ships.

OTHER SIGHTS

Casa Rosada, the Pink House, just inside the entrance to El Morro, was built in 1812 for the Spanish army, and is now an artisans' center.

La Casita (the Little House) was built in 1937 for the Department of Agriculture and now houses the **Puerto Rico Tourism Company's Information Center** (☎ 722-1709), which is open daily. An outdoors craft market is held there every weekend from 11am to 10pm. On the first Saturday of every month, local artists and musicians perform and exhibit their works.

Casa Don Q, in front of Pier One, is an exhibit featuring rum production with a souvenir shop. It is open daily from 9am to 6pm. ☎ 977-1720.

La Fortaleza is the official home and residence of the Governor of

Puerto Rico. It was built in 1530's and is the oldest Governor's mansion in continuous use in the New World. The impressive building was originally constructed as a defence against raiding Carib Indians as well as being the Governor's official residence. The tower and gate date back to the original construction, although much of the rest of the building was rebuilt in the 1800s. The beautiful chapel with its intricate mosaic tiling had both spiritual and secular uses, as it was also used to store the island's gold. La Fortaleza is now a World Heritage Site and there are guided tours in both English and Spanish between 9am and 3.30pm Monday to Friday ☎ 721-7000.

El Arsenal was built in 1800, and was the last place to be occupied by the Spanish on the island. After the **Spanish-American War** in 1898, the US Peace Commission agreed that Spanish troops could stay in the building until ships arrived to evacuate them home. The building now has three galleries that stage regular exhibitions.

Plazoleta de la Rogativa, which stands on a hill, is dedicated to a Spanish bishop who led a torchlight religious procession in 1797, said to have frightened off an attack by British troops.

The **San Juan Cathedral** is one of the oldest places of Christian worship in the Western Hemisphere. Work on the cathedral started in 1540 and it is one of the rare buildings incorporating true medieval architectural elements in the New World, with its four vaulted Gothic ceilings. It is noted for its circular staircase, and many historic religious artifacts. The body of Ponce de León lies in a marble tomb, having been moved here in 1913, and his coat of arms hangs over the altar. Close to the tomb is the mummy of San Pío, a Roman Catholic martyr, buried in 1862. The cathedral is open daily from 8.30am to 4pm ☎ 722-0861.

Opposite the cathedral is the former 17th century Carmelite Convent with its massive wooden doors, originally intended to keep the world out. The beautifully restored building is to become the city's new **Fine Arts Museum**.

San José Church is the second oldest church in the Western Hemisphere and was the family church of Ponce de León and his descendants. It is noted for its vaulted ceilings, statute of Christ and processional floats. It is open from 8.30am to 4pm Monday to Saturday and for services on Sunday ☎ 725-7501.

Capilla del Cristo, the small Christ Chapel, is at the end of Cristo Street, and with its silver altar, is dedicated to the Christ of Miracles. It was originally built in thanks by a young man whose life was saved in 1753 when the horse he was riding at full gallop stopped just before plunging over the city wall. It was later expanded and is open on Tuesday from 10am to 3.30pm. Next door is the small Parque de las Palomas (pigeon park).

The Casino is one of Old San Juan's grandest structures and was built around 1912 as the Casino de Puerto Rico, one of the most fashionable meeting places for San Juan's high society. The exterior of the building looks more like a Louis X1V chateau with its copper cupola, and the interior is just as impressive with magnificent ballroom, ornate plasterwork and huge chandelier. The building, now restored and

Catedral de San Juan, Old San Juan

Barcardi Rum Distillery, Cataño

43

renamed as the Manuel Pavía Fernández Reception Center, is used for official functions by the State Department and is not open to the public.

Still open to the public is the **Tapia Theatre**, one of the oldest theatres in the Western Hemisphere. It was built in 1832 from public subscription and by levying a tax on bread and imported spirits, and still stages plays, opera and ballet.

At the top of Cristo Street is the **Seminario Conciliar de San Ildefonso** that was built in 1832 as a college for outstanding students, a role it still performs. In 1987 the building received the Preservation Trust Award from the US National Trust for Historic Preservation, the first project of its kind in Puerto Rico to win this award and recognition. Of special interest is the neo-classical chapel.

The Capitol, home to the island's legislature, dates from the 1920s, and houses the offices of the senators in one wing, and the representatives in the other. A magnificent rotunda tops the impressive building. On display inside is the island's constitution approved in 1952. There are free guided tours on weekdays.

City Hall, opposite the **Plaza de Armas**, was started in 1604 but was not finally completed because of constant extensions until 1789. The double arcade and two towers were modeled on Madrid City Hall. At the San Francisco Street entrance there is a tourist information center. The Plaza de Armas was the city's main square in the 17th century and gets its name because it was where the soldiers and citizen militia trained. It later became a fashionable meeting place, and the four statues that still grace the square, represent the four seasons.

The late neo-classical **Provincial Assembly Building** was built in the late 1890s, and Puerto Rico's first elected parliament met there on 17 July 1898. The building, noted for its elegance with arches and cloister-like interior, has recently been restored and now houses the Puerto Rican State Department.

The recently opened Wyndham Old San Juan Hotel and Casino is part of a major restoration project including residential and commercial areas and parking in San Juan's waterfront district. The hotel has 242 rooms, gourmet restaurants, bars, a pool and health club, with adjoining casino and conference facilities.

Plazuela de la Rogativa is at the top of the hill at the end of Recinto Oeste and features a bronze statue by Lindsay Daen of a Bishop and his followers carrying torches. According to legend, the Bishop marched his followers up the hill in 1797 during an attack by British troops. The attackers thought the column of men were reinforcements and fled.

OTHER THINGS TO SEE AND DO AROUND SAN JUAN:

San Juan Beaches: The beach resort of San Juan runs from Old San Juan and takes in the districts of **Condado, Miramar, Ocean Park** and **Isla Verde**. Here sun and fun tourists can find everything they want, from top class hotels and restaurants, casinos and nightclubs to great, great beaches. There are opportunities for a huge range of sports from tennis and windsurfing, to diving and deep–sea fishing. And, for those who want to shop, there are top name boutiques and duty free shops.

Plaza de Hostos in front of Plaza de la Darsena and close to La Casita, is a great place to view the work of local artists and craftsmen and enjoy some of the island's traditional 'fast food' snacks.

The **Bacardí Distillery** is the world's largest rum distillery, and is conveniently reached by ferry from San Juan Bay. There are daily tours through its 127 acres (51 hectares), where 100,000 gallons (almost 22,000 liters) of rum can be distilled daily. There are free rum drinks, as well as a gift shop where you can buy a wide range of souvenirs, and bottles of rum. The rum prices are much lower than you would pay back home in a store, and some of the specialist rums are not available off the island. The distillery is open from 8.30am to 4.30pm Monday to Saturday ☎ 788-8400.

The distillery is in the suburbs of Cataño, one of the many municipalities that make up sprawling metropolitan San Juan. Close by is the **Barrilito Rum Plant** with its 200 year-old great house, and 150 year-old windmill, both listed as National Historic Places.

To the west is Bayamón, which although part of metropolitan San Juan, is also Puerto Rico's fastest growing city in its own right. It has a charming historic zone with plaza, church and shopping mall. Nearby, the **Luis A Ferré Science Park** on Route 167 has five museums on geology, archaeology, transportation (including an extensive collection of antique cars) and natural sciences, health and space with a planetarium. They are open from 8am to 4pm Wednesday to Friday, and from 10am to 6pm at the weekend ☎ 740-6868.

There are also US rockets on display, antique cars, a zoo and a boating lake.

Its **Central Park** has many historical buildings in the landscaped gardens. It is open daily from 8am to 5pm ☎ 798-8191. You can also visit the **Francisco Oller Art and History Museum** in the former City Hall. It is open Monday to Friday from 8am to 4pm. ☎ 785-6010.

To the south is **Río Piedras**, locally known as University City, which was founded in 1714 but which has been part of San Juan since 1951. It is worth visiting for the **Botanical Garden**, which is part of the Agricultural Experiment Station at the University of Puerto Rico. The 75-acre (30 hectare) gardens have hundreds of species of native, tropical plants. One area of the garden alone boasts more than 30,000 orchids, and the palm garden has more than 125 species. The herbarium has a collection of more than 36,000 samples. The gardens, tucked away on the south side of the junctions of Highway 1 and Route 847, are open daily from 9am to 4.30pm with guided tours available. ☎ 250-0000.

Rio Piedras also boasts the largest market on the island, and apart from produce such as fruit and vegetables, you can also buy medicinal herbs that have been used as 'bush' medicine for centuries.

Guaynabo, to the south of the city, is the site of the island's first settlement at Caparra, and you can visit the **Caparra Ruins** and **Museum of the Conquest and Colonization of Puerto Rico** off Highway 2. It is open from 8.30 am to 4.30pm Tuesday to Saturday ☎ 781-4795.

• GREATER SAN JUAN •

Because there are hundreds of eateries in Greater San Juan, this is only a selection of what is available. If you feel a restaurant merits inclusion please let us know.

Amadeus $$
Carib/International,
106 San Sebastian,
☎ 723-7303

Amanda's Café $$
Mexican, 424 Norzagaray
☎ 722-0187

Aquavira $$
Seafood, 364 Fortaleza,
☎ 977-2329

Bossa Nova $$-$$$
Brazilian, 358 Fortaleza
☎ 722-0093

Butterfly People $$
Steaks, 152 Fortaleza
☎ 723-2432

Cafe Berlin $-$$
Healthy fare,
407 San Francisco
☎ 722-5205

Casa Borinquen $$
Carib, 109 San Sebastian
☎ 722-7070

Chaumière $$
French, 367 Tetuán
☎ 722-3330

Chef Marisol $$
Italian, 202 Cristo
☎ 725-7475

Dragon Fly $$
Asian/Latin, 364 Fortaleza
☎ 977-3886

Hard Rock Café $-$$
American,
253 Recinto Sur
☎ 724-7625

Mallorquina $$
Local-Spanish,
207 San Justo
☎ 722-3261

Parrot Club $$
New Latin Cuisine,
363 Fortaleza
☎ 725-7370

Patio del Nispero $-$$
American-deli,
Hotel El Convento
☎ 723-9260

Sala $$$ Tropical
Gourmet, 317 Fortaleza.
☎ 724-4797

Tantra $$
Indian/Indo'Latino,
356 La Fortaleza
☎ 977-8141

Trois Cent Onze $$-$$$
French, 311 Fortaleza
☎ 725-7959

Yukiyú $$-$$$
Japanese,
311 Recinto Sur
☎ 722-1423

In Greater San Juan

Ájili Mójili $-$$ Excellent local fare, Canario By The Lagoon Hotel, Condado
☎ 725-9195

Allegro $$
Italian, 1350 Franklin D. Roosevelt Ave. Puerto Nuevo
☎ 273-9055

Al Salam $$
Arabic, 239 Franklin D. Roosevelt Ave. Hato Rey
☎ 751-6296

Antonio $$
Spanish, 1406 Magdalena, Condado
☎ 723-7567

Augusto's Cuisine $$
Italian, Excelsior Hotel,
Miramar
☎ 725-7700

Aurorita $$
Mexican, 303 De Diego,
Puerto Nuevo
☎ 783-2899

Back Street Hong Kong $$
Chinese, San Juan Hotel,
Isla Verde
☎ 791-1224

Borinquen Brewing Co.
$$ Carib/American,
4899 Isla Verde Ave
☎ 268-1900

**Buenas Ayres Bar
and Grill, $$**
Argentinian,
56 Condada Ave
☎ 725-1818

Carli Café $$
International, San Justo and Recinto Sur, named after owner/pianist Carli Munoz
☎ 725-4927

Caruso $$
Italian, 1104 Ashford,
Condado
☎ 723-6876

Casa Condado $$-$$$
Carib/Seafood, 60
Condada Ave,
☎ 723-8193

Casa Dante $$-$$$
Carib/International, 39
Isla Verde Ave
☎ 726-7310

Cathay $$
Chinese, 410 Ponce de
León, Puerta de Tierra
☎ 722-6695

Chart House $$
Spanish-seafood,
1214 Ashford
☎ 728-0110

Chayote $$
Carib/International, 603
Mirimar Ave.
☎ 722-9385

Cielito Lindo $$ Mexican,
1108 Magdalena Ave,
Condado
☎ 723-5597

Compostela $$
Spanish-International,
106 Condado, Santurce ☎
724-6088

El Zipperle $$$
European, 325 Franklin
D. Roosevelt Ave
Hato Rey
☎ 751-4335

Great Taste $$-$$$
Oriental,
1018 Ashford Ave
☎ 721-8111

Green House $$
Italian, Dutch Inn and
Towers, Condado
☎ 725-4036

Havana's Café $$-$$$
Carib/Seafood,
409 Del Parque St
☎ 725-0888

Howard Johnson's $$
American, Isla Verde,
☎ 982-3991

José José $$
Carib/International, 1110
Magdalena
☎ 725-8496

Jules $$
Portuguese, 301 Cruz
☎ 724-6257

La Casona $$
Spanish-International,
609 San Jorge, Santurce
☎ 727-2717

Margarita $$
Mexican, 1013 Roosevelt,
Puerto Nuevo
☎ 781-8452

Marina del Curro $$
Spanish-Seafood, 11
Marginal, Isla Verde
☎ 728-3628

Marisqueria La Dorada $$
Island specialties, 1105
Magdalena Ave
☎ 722-9583

**Metropol $$ Local-
Continental**
Highway 37 Isla Verde
☎ 791-4046

Passagio $$$
European, Inter
Continental
☎ 791-5000

Piccola Fontana $$
Italian, Wyndham El San
Juan Hotel, Isla Verde
☎ 791-0966

Playita $$ American,
Playa Hotel, Isla Verde
☎ 791-1115

Ramiro's $$
Italian-Spanish, 1106
Magdalena, Condado
☎ 721-9049

Restaurant Uno, $$$
Argentinian, 1210
Valdorioty de Castro
☎ 721-5572

**Ruth's Chris
Steak House $$**
Steaks, Inter-Continental
☎ 791-6100

St. Moritz $$
International, Regency
Hotel, Condado
☎ 721-0999

La Tasca $$
Seafood, 54 Muñoz Rivera,
Puerta de Tierra
☎ 722-2410

Tiramisú $$
Italian,
Baldorioty de Castro
☎ 268-5002

Tony Roma's $$
Spanish, Condado Plaza
Hotel, Condado
☎ 722-0322

Torreblanca $$
International, 1110
Magdalena, Condado
☎ 725-8496

Urdin $$$
Carib/International, 1105
Magdalena Ave
☎ 724-0420

Veranda $$
International,
Inter-Continental,
Isla Verde
☎ 791-1000

Via Appia $$
Italian, 1350 Ashford,
Condado
☎ 725-8711

Wasabi $$
Japanese, 1372 Ashford Ave
☎ 724-6411

Yuan $$
Chinese
255 Ponce de León,
Hato Rey
☎ 766-0666

($ Inexpensive, $$ Moderate , $$$ Expensive).

47

ISLAND TOURS

There are a number of options for touring the island depending on whether you are staying in one hotel or moving around. All the following routes start and end either in San Juan or Ponce. The layout of the island roads, however, with its combination of coastal routes and trans-island roads, means that all the tours can easily be adapted to suit your particular needs and time constraints. Some are suggested as day trips but are even better if spread over two days. For each of the trips it is essential to have a good road map. Once you leave the main highways, there is often a choice of routes between towns and sights, and the map will give you added flexibility.

TRAVELLING TIME

The following are average traveling times and distances from San Juan: Aguadilla 2 hours, 81 miles (130km), Arecibo 1 hour, 48 miles (77km), Bayamón 15 minutes, 8 miles (13km), Cayey 45 minutes, 30 miles (48km), Comerío 1 hour, 25 miles (40km), Dorado 30 minutes, 19 miles (30km), Fajardo 45 minutes, 34 miles (54km), Guayama 1 hour 30 minutes, 44 miles (70km), Humacao 40 minutes, 34 miles (54km), Mayagüez 2 hours 30 minutes, 98 miles (160km), Ponce 1 hour 30 minutes, 70 miles (112km), Salinas 1 hour 10 minutes, 46 miles (74km), San Germán 2 hours 30 minutes, 105 miles (168km), San Sebastián 2 hours, 76 miles (122km), and Yabucoa 1 hour, 43 miles (69km).

TOUR ONE (120 MILES - 184KM)

From San Juan head north towards the coast and the residential area of Santurce, home of the **Puerto Rico Art Museum** and **Luis A. Ferré Performing Arts Center**. The Art Museum, 299 de Diego Ave, has a number of world class exhibits, interactive galleries, theater, and a five-acre garden with lakes and trails featuring more than 100,000 plants. The gardens also contain sculptures by local artists. The Museum is open Tuesday to Saturday from 10am to 5pm and on Sunday from 11am to 5pm. ☎ 977-6277. The Arts Center on Ponce de Leon Ave. has three concert halls ☎ 724-4747.

Continue on Highway 26 to Carolina. Across the Laguna La Torrecilla is the **Piñones Forest**, which contains Puerto Rico's largest mangrove forest. This is an area of beautiful unspoiled beaches, huge coconut estates and saltwater lagoons that teem with bird life. Canóvanas is home to El Comandante horse racing track and La Antigua Ceiba, a 300 year old ceiba tree on Palmer Street. The fastest route to the east coast is Highway 3. There is not much to see except speeding traffic, but if you want to get about quickly, take this dual lane highway and detour off to take in selected sights along the way.

A new attraction off highway 187, is a 6 mile long boardwalk known as the **Paseo Pinones Recreational Trail**. You can rent bikes. The small coastal town of **Loíza** is famous for the **San Patricio Church**, one of the oldest on the island, started in 1645 and completed in 1670. Loíza also has a high percentage of African descendants, and African culture and traditions are still strong.

The area between Río Grande and Luquillo is now a fast growing resort district. It is home to the 600-room luxury Westin Rio Mar Beach Resort and Country Club (☎ 888-6000) and Ocean Villas, as well as the Berwind Country Club (☎ 876-3056) and Bahia Beach Plantation Resort (☎ 256-5600). Between them, the resorts boast four championship golf courses. Off the 965 is the Rio Grande Plantation Eco Resort.

You can detour inland on Route 191 off Highway 3 to visit the **Luquillo Mountain Range** and **El Yunque Peak** at the center of a huge 28,000-acre (11,200 hectare) rainforest in the mountains. It is part of the **Caribbean National Forest** that was first established by the Spanish crown in 1876, making it one of the Western Hemisphere's oldest natural reserves. In 1903 President Roosevelt declared it a national park and it is still the only tropical rainforest in the US National Park System.

EL YUNQUE RAINFOREST

El Yunque is well worth exploring and even if you do not plan to go on a full tour of the island, it makes a great day trip from San Juan that is only 45 minutes away via Highway 3 and Route 191. It is one of the highlights of any trip to Puerto Rico and most hotels and sightseeing companies offer guided tours. If driving yourself be careful as the road up into the mountains is steep, narrow in places and very twisting. Route 191 is only open from dawn to dusk. Remember though that it is a rainforest and there can be downpours at any time, so bring a waterproof jacket or poncho and wear non-slip footwear.

It rarely rains for long, however, and you will quickly dry off, and there are a number of shelters scattered around the reserve.

As you climb into the mountains, you can see virgin forests that look the same today as when Columbus first landed 500 years ago.

It has been estimated that about 100 billion gallons of rain fall each year on the forest, which contains more than 240 varieties of trees and other flowering plants. Its Spanish name comes from its distinctive anvil shape. El Yunque consists of four distinct forest zones and is home to 240 species of tropical trees, flowers and wildlife. There are 20 kinds of orchid and 50 varieties of fern, and miniature tree frogs (Eleutherodactylus portoricensis) whose distinctive 'coquí' cry gives them their name.

It is a magnificent area of lush, tropical vegetation, waterfalls, wild orchids, giant ferns, towering tabonuco (Dacryodes excelsa) trees and sierra (Euterpe globosa) palms. Tropical birds include the magnificent Puerto Rican parrot (Amazona vittata), once nearly extinct and now making a comeback thanks to a concerted conservation and breeding program. Other rare creatures include the Puerto Rican boa, which can grow up to seven feet (2m) long. There are also 26 animal species found in the forest and nowhere else in the world.

WALKING TRAILS

This makes it a naturalist's as well as a photographer's paradise, and there are dozens of well marked walking trails to allow you to explore in safety. The walks, all detailed on a free map, are graded according to difficulty, and the most strenuous is the rugged six mile-long (10km) **El Toro Trail** which passes through all four forest zones, to its peak at 3523 feet (1074m). **The Big Tree Trail** is an easy walk to the beautiful **La Mina Falls**, and just off the road is **La Coca Falls**, a sheet of water that cascades down mossy cliffs, and an observation tower for easy viewing. Nearby, the **Sierra Palm Visitor and Interpretive Service Center** offers maps and information, and arranges talks, programs of activities and guided tours of the forest. If you are interested in natural history or really want to learn more about the forest and its

La Mina Falls, El Yunque Rain Forest

wildlife, it does pay to go on a guided tour, or hire your own guide. You will have things pointed out that you would almost certainly miss if you are on your own. Also close to the summit of the tallest peak is the popular El Yunque Restaurant where you can eat within earshot of the roaring **La Mina River**. Camping is allowed in many parts of the park but a free permit is required ☎ 887-2875 or 766-5335.

The new tropical forest center **El Portal del Yunque**, explains the management and conservation of tropical forests, what can be seen and what there is to do. The center has three areas, an interpretive visitor center, an environmental education facility for local school children, and a tropical forest management training center for Latin American resource managers. ☎ 888-1880.

LUQUILLO

Return to Highway 3 and then turn off for **Luquillo** where you can have a swim at the popular and beautiful public beach, one of the finest on the island. Luquillo is a Spanish version of the Taíno word Yukiyú, the Indian god who, according to legend, was supposed to inhabit El Yunque. Luquillo, with its soft white sand and fringe of majestic coconut palms is a near-perfect tropical beach stretching for almost a mile (1.6km). It is a lovely place for a picnic although you can try local delicacies from the food stalls along the road just past the beach entrance. The beach is very popular with locals at the weekend.

For real fast food, stop by one of the roadside stalls and buy freshly picked fruit or pick out a green coconut for a refreshing drink. The vendor will slice the top of the coconut off and make a hole so you can drink the liquid inside. When you have finished drinking, hand the coconut back, and the vendor will split the nut in half and chop off a sliver of the hard shell which you use as a spoon to gouge out the white soft jelly inside. Always ask for

Icacos Cay

a really green coconut because the liquid is sweeter, and the jelly softer.

There are lockers and showers that are available from 9am to 5pm daily except Monday. If you don't have lots of time to explore the country, a day trip from San Juan spending the morning in El Yunque, and lunch and the afternoon at Luquillo makes a great day out. On the east side of Luquillo beach there is 'Sea Without Barriers', a wheelchair accessible area that allows access into the sea.

Continue east on Highway 3 and then turn off for Fajardo where you can catch the ferry to Culebra and Vieques. If you plan to take your car, you must make a reservation at least a week in advance and earlier in the high season.

Fajardo is now a busy and popular area for sailing and diving, with several marinas, including Puerto del Rey Marina, the largest in the Caribbean, excellent restaurants and

the Puerto Real ferry terminal to visit Culebra and Vieques. There are a number of other small, secluded and unpopulated islands offshore - Icacos, Lobos and Palominos - which can be visited, and whose clear waters are great for snorkeling. There is a lovely public beach at Seven Seas, and you can buy the freshest of fish at Las Croabas Bay as the fishermen come ashore with their catches. There are several good restaurants in the area, including those at the spectacular El Conquistador resort.

To the north on Route 987, is the Cabezas de San Juan Nature Reserve on the northeastern tip of the island. The reserve opened in 1991 and its 316 acres (126 hectares) contain seven very different ecological systems - forest, mangroves, lagoons, beaches, cliffs, offshore waters and coral reefs. Boardwalk trails wind through the mangroves, dry forests and Laguna Grande bioluminescent lagoon. From the promontories and rocky beach you can spot ospreys, sea turtles and an occasional manatee. Visitors can also visit the 19th century restored Spanish Colonial **El Faro Lighthouse** in neo-classic style from whose observation deck distant Caribbean islands can be spotted including St. Thomas in the US Virgin Islands. The lighthouse has been in continuous use since 1882. The reserve, which includes nature center and archaeological excavations, is open by reservation only from Wednesday to Sunday. You will get a conducted tour of the reserve by an experienced guide who will make sure you get maximum enjoyment and don't miss a thing. ☎ 722-5882. South of Fajardo is **Roosevelt Roads**, the largest U.S. naval base in the world.

THE OFFSHORE ISLANDS

The islands of Culebra and Vieques are noted for their beauty, secluded white sandy beaches, clear waters, coral reefs and fresh seafood. **Vieques Air Link** and **Isla Nena Air Services** provide air links with the islands and there are regular ferry sailings from Fajardo.

CULEBRA

Culebra lies due east of Fajardo and is surrounded by a cluster of more than 20 tiny unpopulated islands or cays. Tens of thousands of years ago massive sea turtles came ashore to lay their eggs. These huge sea creatures, the ancestors of today's leatherback turtles, weighed two tons and more. More recently, the remote island which covers 25 square miles (65sq.km) made an ideal refuge for pirates, who could

hide out in the sheltered bays and among the cays, and at the beginning of the 20th century a naval base was established on the island, while much of the rest of the land was declared a **National Wildlife Refuge** by President Theodore Roosevelt in 1909. Today the offshore waters offer fabulous diving and snorkeling in the warm, clear unpolluted waters, while the island itself has a small, laid back tourist industry and a resident population of about 2,000. The rugged countryside is great for hiking and bird watching, and **Flamenco Beach** outside the main town of Dewey is fabulous. **The Polvorín Museum** on route 250 at El Campamento, combines an art and history museum and exhibits by local artists. It is open Monday to Friday from 8am to noon.

VIEQUES

Vieques is the larger of the two islands to the south of Culebra and has a population of about 8,000. It measures roughly 25 miles (16km) by five miles (8km) and was at first the home of the gentle Arawak Indians, and then a hide-away for pirates in the 17th century. Because of its strategic location, the island was fought over by the European colonial powers, but it remained in Spanish hands until it was ceded to the U.S., along with the rest of Puerto Rico, at the end of the 19th century. The Spanish built the fort in the main town of Isabel Segunda, and the lighthouse was built more than 100 years ago to signal the harbor entrance. Both have been restored and are now museums. The fort, **Fortín del Conde de Mirasol**, was the last built by Spain in the New World and now houses an art and history museum open

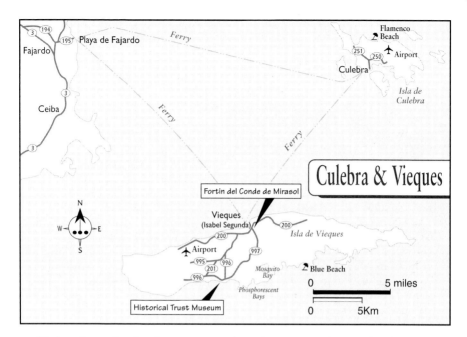

Culebra & Vieques

Map labels:
- Fajardo
- 194
- 195 Playa de Fajardo
- 3
- Ferry
- Flamenco Beach
- 251
- 250
- Airport
- Culebra
- Ceiba
- 3
- Isla de Culebra
- Ferry
- Ferry
- Fortin del Conde de Mirasol
- N / W–E / S
- Vieques (Isabel Segunda)
- 200
- 200
- Isla de Vieques
- Airport
- 995
- 996
- 201
- 996
- 997
- Mosquito Bay
- Blue Beach
- Phosphorescent Bays
- Historical Trust Museum
- 0 ... 5 miles
- 0 ... 5Km

Wednesday to Sunday from 10am to 4pm. ☎ 741-1717. There is also the **Conservation and Historical Trust Museum** in a restored sugar mill at Esperanza, the small fishing village on the south coast that has the liveliest night life. The Museum highlights the island's early history and is open from 11am to 4pm, Tuesday to Sunday ☎ 741-8850. The town of Esperanza used to rely on the sugar cane industry, but is now a tourist and fishing center. The nearby Sombé (Sun Bay) public beach has camping and picnic sites. Today the island is popular with snorkelers, especially off **Blue Beach**, and famous for the phosphorescent **Mosquito Bay**. Camping is allowed on the island at Sombé, but a permit, which is free, is required. Because of the virgin reefs, the island is popular with divers and many dive schools on Puerto Rico run trips there. The US Navy still controls large areas of the island, and that continued with its offshore practice bombing is a source of continuing controversy.

If staying on the mainland, follow the east coast down through **Ceiba** to **Naguabo** with its lovely beaches and the **El Salto de Rio Blanco Falls**. Offshore is a cay known locally as **Monkey Island**. It is the University of **Puerto Rico Medical School's Caribbean Primate Research Center**. While you can't land on the island, there are boat tours that allow you to get close. The waters are also excellent for snorkeling. **Naguabo Plaza** is the second largest on the island.

You can detour south to visit **Humacao** along the newly opened stretch of autopista 52 that runs south to **Yabucoa**. Set in sugar cane country this is another fast growing resort area. Visit the Casa Roig museum and cultural center in a building designed in the 1920s by architect Antonin Nechodoma, a disciple of Frank Lloyd Wright. It is open Sunday to Friday from 10am to 4pm. ☎ 852-3066.

Just south of Humacao is the **Palmas del Mar Resort**, which covers 2,750 acres (1100 hectares), has more

than 3,000 coconut palms and is the largest resort on the island. There are more than 24 excellent dive sites within five miles (8km) of Humacao, many along the one mile (1.6km) long **Basslet Reef**. Or head inland for another visit to the Caribbean National Forest, before continuing west on Highway 30 to Las Piedras and Juncos to connect with Highway 1 which runs north back into San Juan. **Las Piedras** is noted for its artisans and local crafts. **The local history museum** is open Monday to Friday 8am to 4.30pm. ☎ 733-9360. **Cueva del India** is a national historic monument with more than 150 petroglyphs. Junco's historic district contains many fine old buildings including the City Hall, Library and Old Hospital. The **Teatro Junqueño** is another historic monument used for cultural events and folklore presentations.

On the way you back to San Juan you can visit Lake Loíza and Trujillo Alto.

E A T I N G   O U T

* MG denotes membership of Mesones Gastronómicos. To qualify, a restaurant must promote the best of Puerto Rican cuisine at reasonable prices and with true Puerto Rican hospitality.

Fajardo

A la Banda $$
Seafood/International,
Hwy 3 on the waterfront.
☎ 860-9162

Anchor's Inn $$
Seafood-Steaks,
Route 987
☎ 863-7200 MG

Pasion $$-$$$
Carib/International,
Puerto Chico Hwy 987
☎ 863-3502

Rosa's Seafood $$
Seafood, 536 Tablazo,
Puerto Real
☎ 863-0213 MG

Gurabo

Sevilla $$-$$$
Carib/International,
Hwy 189
☎ 737-3259

Humacao

Aji $$ Carib
Hwy 3 and Road 906
☎ 850-3500

Candelero Hotel $$
Local-International,
Palmas del Mar Resort
☎ 852-3450

Chez Daniel $$
Seafood, Hwy 3 and
Road 906
☎ 852 6000 MG

Marie's $$
Seafood-Steaks, Highway 3
☎ 852-5471MG

Paradise Seafood $$
Seafood, Highway 3
☎ 852-1180

Tulio's Seafood $$
Seafood, Aduana
☎ 850-1840 MG

Juncos

El Tenedor $$
Seafood-deli, 1 Emilia
Príncipe
☎ 734-6573 MG

Luquillo

Víctor's Place $$
Seafood, 2 Jesús T. Piñero
☎ 889-5705

Río Grande

El Dajao $$ Island
specialties, Road 191
☎ 888-6716

Las Vegas $$
Local-Seafood, Route 191
☎ 887-2526 MG

Vieques

Casa del Francés $$
Local cuisine, Route 996
☎ 741-3751

Chez Shack $$
Carib/International,
Route 995
☎ 741-2175

TOUR TWO (160 MILES 256KM)

Take expressway 52 south heading for Caguas which has a Cathedral and several small museums. See how hand rolled cigars are made at the **Museo del Tabaco Herminio Torres**. It is open Tuesday to Friday from 8.30am to 4pm and on Saturday from 8.30am to 3pm. ☎ 744-2960.

Then head for Cayey but turn left onto Route 184, for the Carite Reserve Forest. It covers 6,000 acres (2,400 hectares), with **Cerro La Santa** the highest peak at 3000 feet (915m). The road runs through spectacular scenery, through tunnels of towering bamboo and fantastic mountain vistas. **The Nuestra Madre**, a Catholic retreat set in lovely gardens with royal palms, mahogany and eucalyptus trees, sits on another of the reserve's mountain peaks. Every Easter, thousands of pilgrims make their way to the retreat where there is a shrine where the Virgin Mary is said to have appeared. The grounds are open to the public and offer a delightful place for a picnic with spectacular

views, and afterwards you can drive to **Charco Azul** (Blue Pool) and have a swim in the blue waters of the large natural pool, one of the main attractions of the reserve. The pool is about one mile inland from the roadside parking area.

It is easiest to drive south on Route 184 to Patillas and head north again through the forests and mountains on Route 181 to connect with Route 182 that runs east to Yabucoa. **Central Roig** is an historic sugar plantation, one of six huge estates that used to operate in the area. ☎ 893-1000. You can then head south on Route 3 to Maunabo and the lighthouse at Punta Tuna.

Then follow the south coast round on Highway 3 to Punta Guilarte, detouring off the main road to take in the sights as necessary.

Both Arroyo and Guayama just inland, used to rely heavily on smuggling. There are now guided tours of Arroyo aboard a trolley bus or a restored train, the Tren del Sur de Arroyo (☎ 271-1574). **The Museo Antigua Aduana** traces the city's history. It is open Monday to

Friday from 9 to 11.45am and 1 to 4.15 pm. ☎ 839-8096. The Casa Cautiño museum in Guayama is also worth visiting. It is in a beautiful Creole house built in 1887, and has period furnishings and effects of the Cautiño family who lived there. It is open from 9am to 4.30pm Tuesday to Saturday and 10am to 4.30pm on Sunday ☎ 864-9083. The town has a fine arts center open 1pm to 6.30 pm Wednesday to Friday and 10am to 6pm at weekends ☎ 864-7765, as well as good public beaches. **The Jobos Bay Nature reserve**, take Highways 707 or 705 off Highway 3 It is open daily from 7.30am to 4pm ☎ 864-0105. This stretch of road is noted for its 'lechoneras' or food stalls offering local delicacies, such as pit-roasted pork (lechón asao), black pudding (morcillas), tripe (mondongo), and white cheese served with green glased papaya (lechosa con queso blanco).

You can visit Aguirre and can then take either Highway 1 or the expressway north back to San Juan via Caguas, or for a very long day, continue westwards along the south coast to **Ponce**.

If continuing to Ponce, it is worth a detour on Highway 153 and then 14 to visit Coamo. It was the main center in the south before Ponce took over, and it is still one of the island's largest towns. It is famous for its thermal springs which attracted the Taíno Indians long before the first Europeans arrived. According to legend, it was the fountain of youth sought by Ponce de León but many other springs on the island also lay claim to this. The town has a fine square, 18th century church, many old buildings and a museum which portrays life at the

end of the 19th century. It is open weekdays from 8am to 4pm ☎ 825-1150.

EATING OUT

Caguas

La Cántara $$
Carib/seafood, Degetau St
☎ 743-0220

El Paraíso $$
Local-Seafood-Italian, Highway 1
☎ 747-2012 MG

Cayey

El Meson de Jorge $$
Local-Seafood, Highway 1
☎ 263-2800 MG

Jájome Terrace $$
Local-French, Highway 15
☎ 738-4016

Sand and Sea Inn $$
Steak, Route 715
☎ 738-9086

Coamo

Baños de Coamo $$
Local-International, Route 546
☎ 825-2239 MG

Maunabo

Los Bohíos $$
Seafood-Steaks,
Route 760
☎ 861-2545

TOUR THREE (220 MILES-352KM)

Take the toll Luis A. Ferré Expressway (52) south from San Juan. This trip can be completed as part of a very long day but is better done over two or more leisurely days. It pays to take the expressway as Ponce can be reached in less than two hours. If you leave San Juan early enough, you may run into fog which clings to the valleys in the Central Mountains, but the heat of the sun usually quickly burns the fog off. If you want to take a slower, more scenic road to Ponce, head west out of San Juan on Hwy 22 to **Manatí**, and then take road 149 south through **Toro Negro**. This tour, however, returns along this scenic route, so the toll highway is suggested as the fastest way to get to Ponce.

SALINAS

If taking the toll expressway, continue to the south coast and head for **Salinas**, one of the island's newest dive centers with the mangrove swamps and nearby Cayo Media Luna great for snorkeling. Salinas is home of Mojo Isleño, a spicy sauce that is excellent with fish and seafood. There are several good beaches along this stretch of coastline - **Playa Santa Isabel**, **Playa Córdoba** and **Playa Salinas**. The church of **Nuestra Señora de las Mercedes** in Plaza de Recreo, is a national historic monument.

Before you arrive in Salinas you pass the Puerto Rico International Speedway and south of this off highway 3 is the information enter for the newly opened **Jobos Bay Nature Reserve**. It has hiking and kayak trails through the mangrove swamps, salt flats and a string of small cays. Boats and kayaks can be rented.

Inland on 149 is Juana Diaz, site of the Three King's Monument and home of the famous and traditional event that takes place annually on January 6. You can also visit **El Salto**

de Collores, a picturesque waterfall. Overlooking the area is the mountaintop sanctuary of **Santuario Schoenstatt** reached by taking highways 14 and 574.

PONCE

Then continue to Ponce. Puerto Rico's second largest city, with a population of around 300,000, is about 90 minutes by car from San Juan, and is another must. Ponce's Mercedita Airport runway has recently been widened for wide-bodied jets, and there are direct international flights from a number of US cities. Ponce's port facilities are currently undergoing a $40 million upgrade.

Ponce on the Caribbean with its yesteryear charm and gentler pace, is a complete contrast from modern, bustling San Juan on the Atlantic. The town was founded in 1692 by the great-grandson of Ponce de León. It is a marvelous place to stroll around, and if you haven't the energy, you can take a horse-drawn carriage, or hop on a trolley. The green and red trolleys leave from City Hall every 20 minutes from 7.30am to 10pm and take in many of the main sights.

For almost the past thirty years, there has been a massive restoration program under way, and more than 600 of its 1,000 historic buildings dating from the mid-1800s have been meticulously restored. There is an incredible mix of architectural styles from neoclassical and art deco to criollo (creole) and colonial Spanish. The blend is very reminiscent of the architecture in the center of Barcelona, with hints of New Orleans, and most dates from the mid-1800s to the 1930s, when the city was enriched by the sugar cane, rum and shipping industries.

Ponce was also the cultural and intellectual heart of the country and attracted poets, artists and musicians, and this legacy continues with the many art galleries, museums, theatres and the surprisingly large number of professional and business schools and universities for its size.

Many of the finest buildings are on the streets that radiate from the grand **Plaza Las Delicias** (Plaza of Delights). The traditional town square is similar to those found in all Spanish colonial towns with its benches and fountains, but few are as grand. The plaza is the place to hang out with its outdoor cafés, and magnificent vistas, especially of the cathedral. Streets running off the plaza include Isabel, Reina, Pabellones and Lolita Tizol, and are interesting for another reason, because in an effort to recreate the true 19th century atmosphere, all telephone and electricity lines have been run underground. It is surprising how it transforms the view, and how much nicer photographs look. The streets have had replica 19th century gas lamps installed and the sidewalks have been trimmed with the distinctive locally-quarried pink marble. Within walking distance of the plaza you can visit:

The Alcaldía or City Hall, built in 1847, is one of the city's two buildings still owned by the Spanish Crown, the other being the **School of Fine Arts**. Calle Isabel (Isabel Street) is one of the city's main residential streets and has a number of magnificent homes reflecting the best of the many different architectural styles to be found throughout Ponce. There are fine examples of European neoclassic, Spanish Colonial, Ponce-Creole, Town Creole, Residential Town Creole, neoclassic Creole and superior neoclassic architecture.

Casa Armstrong-Poventud is one of Ponce's most famous landmarks, and is now home of the tourist information center. It is easy to spot with its caryatid columns facing the cathedral. It was built in 1899 for the founder of the now-extinct Banco de Ponce, and is one of the earliest neoclassic buildings in the city ☎ 844-8240.

Casa Paoli on Mayor Street, was built in 1914, and houses the Puerto Rico Center for Folkloric Research, and was the birthplace of world-renowned operatic tenor Antonio Paoli. It is a lively venue for art exhibitions and other cultural events. It is open Wed to Fri 2-5pm and Sat 11am to 3pm. ☎ 840-4115.

Casa Serrallés is on the corner of Calle Isabel and Calle Salud, and is a fine example of the superior neoclassical-style. Built in 1911 for the Serrallés family, the island's oldest rum making family, the building is now an art studio and gallery under the auspices of the Institute of Puerto Rican Culture ☎ 259-1774.

Casa Wiechers-Villaronga (Casa Reina) is considered the finest example of neo-classical architecture in Ponce. Its owner the architect Alfredo Wiechers designed it in 1912. Wiechers studied architecture in Paris, and after working in Barcelona, returned to Ponce where he designed several buildings, including the original Banco de Ponce and magnificent residences. He was strongly influenced by European-Baroque styles with their elaborate decorations of Ionic columns, moldings, floral garlands, sculptured lions and art nouveau iron railings.

The Cathedral of Our Lady of Guadalupe was named after Ponce's patron saint. The Fiestas Patronales of Our Lady of Guadalupe are held every February and are one of the most colorful fiestas on the island.

The Escuela de Bellas Artes was built for the Spanish Corps of Engineers in 1849 and was then the headquarters of the Spanish Infantry until the American invasion in 1898. Later it was a Court of Justice and then a jail from 1959 until 1987. It now features musical, theatrical and arts workshops and a 600-seat theatre.

Catedral Nt. Sra. de la Guadalupe, Ponce

The Fox Delicias Theatre combines Hollywood Art deco and Mediterranean styles typified by its red tile roof. The 1930's grand cinema is on the north side of Plaza las Delicias, and is now an air-conditioned mini shopping mall and cafe theater. It is a great place to eat with tempting pastries and Puerto Rican specialties such as arroz con pollo, sancocho and rice and beans, and great espresso.

Paseo Tablado La Guancha, outside town by the sea, is where you promenade if you don't want to hang out in the Plaza Las Delicias.

The Museum of the History of Ponce occupies two houses on the corner of Isabel and Mayor streets, and traces the history of the city from the time of the Taíno Indians to the present. Casa Candal Salazar, built in 1911, is regarded as one of Ponce's greatest treasures, incorporating neoclassic and Moorish styles with much decorative detail such as stained glass windows, mosaics, pressed-tin ceilings, fixed jalousies (shutters), wood or iron columns, porch balconies, interior patios and the use of doors as windows. The adjacent building is the equally impressive Casa Zapater, and between them they house ten galleries and exhibition halls. The museum was opened in December 1992 on the 300th anniversary of the founding of the city. It features interactive displays that help visitors orient themselves and locate other attractions. There is also a conservation laboratory, library, souvenir and gift shop, and cafeteria. The museum is open from 10am to 5pm daily except Tuesday. ☎ 844-7071.

The Museum of Puerto Rican Music, 70 Cristina Street, is an historic 19th century Ponceño Creole residence built by Italian-born Juan Bertoli Calderoni, the father of Puerto Rico's neoclassical architectural style. It was the first house in Ponce to have a telephone, was the former home of the Ponce Art Museum and is now a showcase for Puerto Rican music, from pre-Columbian times to the present, including the African musical influence in the bomba and plena, and the danza. Exhibits include Indian, Spanish and African musical instruments. It is open from 9am to noon and 1pm to 5.30pm, Wednesday to Sunday ☎ 844-9722.

The Parque de Bombas Firehouse Museum is one of the city's most cherished monuments. The red and black striped firehouse dates from 1882, and is behind the cathedral on **Plaza Las Delicias**, the main square. It was built for an agricultural and industrial fair exhibition hall in 1882, and the following year became Ponce's, and the island's, first fire station. It remained a fire station until 1990. It is now a museum with historic fire trucks, equipment and memorabilia. It is open from 10am to 6pm daily except Tuesday. Guided tours are available ☎ 284-4141.

Every Sunday night it is the venue for a free concert by the city's municipal band.

Paseo Arias or **Callejón Amor** (Love Lane) is a charming pedestrian passage between two 1920s bank buildings, Banco Popular and Banco Santander on Plaza Las Delicias.

Paseo Atocha is one of Ponce's main shopping streets and now a delightful pedestrian mall, which holds a very lively street festival on the third Sunday of every month.

Edward Durrell Stone, the architect of New York's Museum of Art, designed the modern Ponce Art Museum, on Las Américas Avenue. The museum is sometimes referred to as the **Parthenon of the Antilles,** because the impressive building houses the most extensive art museum in the Caribbean. It was founded in 1959 by former Governor and prominent philanthropist Luis A. Ferré, and houses more than 1,000 paintings, 800 sculptures and 500 prints spanning five centuries, and is especially noted for its late

Renaissance and Baroque works, and 19th century pre-Raphaelite canvasses. It also displays works by many prominent Puerto Rican artists, and there is also a library and three delightful gardens. It is open every day of the week Mon to Sat 10am to 5pm, Sundays 9am to 5pm ☎ 848-0505.

The **Teatro la Perla**, with its six Corinthian columns, is one of the earliest examples of Bertoli's neoclassical structures in Ponce and hosts evening concerts, plays and dances year-round. It was built in 1864 and destroyed by an earth-quake in 1918. It was not rebuilt until 1940 and the theatre, an exact replica of the original, opened in 1941, and is noted for its fine acoustic properties. Visitors are welcome during the day, and you may get a sneak preview of actors rehearsing during the afternoon ☎ 834-4080.

The Serrallés Castle Museum (Museo Castillo Serrallés) is at the end of a scenic drive into the El Vigía Hill and is housed in Castillo Serrallés, a former mansion owned by the founders of the Mercedita sugar mill, the island's oldest rum making family, and makers of Don Q Rum. It was built in the 1930s in Spanish Revival-style, a mix of Spanish and Moorish elements, and the multi-level house is now a museum of family furnishings with displays of the sugar and rum industry. After a short film, you can take a guided tour of the house. It is open from 9.30am to 5pm Tuesday to Thursday, and from 10am to 5.30pm Friday to Sunday ☎ 259-1774.

On top of the hill there is **La Cruceta del Vigía**, a 100-foot (30m) high observation tower.

The Tibes Indian Ceremonial Park (Route 503) is just outside town, and the oldest Indian burial ground in the Antilles. These pre-Columbian Igneri and Taíno Indian sites date from around 700AD, although skeletons unearthed during excavations date back to 200AD. The site contains seven ceremonial bateyes, or ball courts, two dance grounds and a recreated Taíno village. Large upright stones, some of which are marked with petroglyphs, surround the ball courts and the ground was used to play a game, which could have been a forerunner of football. Large stones on the ceremonial dance ground are laid in line with the rays of the sun during the equinox and solstice. It is not known, however, whether these stones had religious or astronomic significance. The museum has exhibits including ceremonial objects, jewelry and pottery. It is open from Tuesday to Sunday 9am to 4pm and bilingual tours are available ☎ 840-2255.

The nearby **Hacienda Buena Vista** is 20 minutes north of Ponce near the small town of Barrio Magueyes on Highway 123, and is a recently restored 19th century coffee plantation and grain mill, which is now open to the public as a museum. The rich smell of coffee from beans drying in trays, still lingers over the sprawling plantation which runs along the Canas River just north of Ponce. The bright red and gray Hacienda Buena Vista, the two-story estate house, and other buildings were built in 1833, and restored during the late 1980s by the Conservation Trust of Puerto Rico. **Salvador de Vives**, a Spaniard who came to Puerto Rico via Venezuela, was responsible for making **Buena Vista** one of the island's most successful plantations, producing coffee, corn, flour and citrus fruit. He was an innovative farmer and realized early on, that the land was too hilly for really economic sugar cane production that was the main crop in the area. Salvador planted a vast range of crops to see which did best and yielded the greatest profits. He planted yams, pineapples, mafafo bananas, cacao, corn and coffee, and all did well. As the other estates continued to grow only sugar cane, he found he had a ready local market for his produce and no problem selling the surplus abroad. He introduced a cotton gin, coffee processing plant and rice milling machine, and the estate fast became one of the most efficient and most mechanized on the island. Salvador's son Carlos established a corn mill in 1853 and the flour was of such good quality, that it was highly sought after even in Spain. The farm owed its survival to the diversity of crops grown, and as world coffee prices dropped, the estate simply stepped up production of citrus for which there was a growing export market. By 1904, the farm had more than 1,000 orange trees.

The property was owned by the Vives family for 150 years and was a working coffee plantation until the 1950s. By studying old photographs and family documents, the Trust, who bought the land in 1984, has been able to faithfully restore the hacienda's buildings and machinery. Today, 80 acres (32 hectares) of the estate's original 500 acres (200 hectares) remain.

The ground floor of the main house is now a museum and contains wonderful old photographs, maps, bills of sale and other exhibits directly relating to the plantation and life on the estate. The first floor

contains the large, spacious bedrooms, all with fine views of the estate. Note the all-wood construction and the use of the local ausubo (manilkara bidentata) wood for termite-resistant beams. The narrow balcony runs round three sides of the house. The first floor also contains the long dining room and living room and the inner patio, which was a common feature in the luxurious houses of San Juan and Venezuela of the day. The kitchen and additional bedrooms run alongside the patio, which opens onto a yard with a rose garden. All the rooms have been restored with authentic period furnishings from the 1850s, and contain many of the family's personal artifacts.

You can explore the great house and mills and see the original water wheels and other 19th century equipment that were in daily use for more than 100 years. They have been faithfully restored down to the last nuts and bolts. The nearby Canas River powered the mid-19th century water wheels and a hydraulic turbine, built by the West Point Foundry in 1853, was used to grind cornmeal. The machinery collection is considered one of the finest in the Western Hemis-phere because so little from this important period of the industrial revolution has survived. Much of the iron used in this machinery was commandeered during the two World Wars and converted for other uses. The Smithsonian Institute in Washington recognized the importance of the machinery collection and has been a major supporter of the restoration project.

The Buena Vista estate, rightly named 'beautiful view', used to be a self-contained community with the great house, outbuildings and mills and former slave quarters which later became the coffee storage and drying shed. The massive masonry storage shed also doubled up as the hurricane shelter. You can stroll along the paths over which wagons once trundled carrying their loads of harvested coffee beans and newly milled corn. Bananas and pineapples grow on the hillsides around the plantation, and the surrounding countryside with its tumbling streams and waterfalls is rich in plant and wildlife, including the Puerto Rican screech owl, mangrove cuckoo and hummingbird. The hacienda is open for conducted tours from Wednesday to Sunday but reservations are required. There are tours at 8.30am, 10.30am, 1.30pm and 3.30pm. ☎ 722-5882.

From Ponce take Highway 14 northeast to Juana Díaz then 149 north to **Lake Guayabal** and **Villalba**. Villalba is a charming mountain town with cobblestone streets and fountains. The Orocovis-Mirador Villalba is an observation tower on route 143 and offering fantastic panoramic views.

Then drive along 149 through the **Central Mountain Range**. This area produces the island's best coffee and has many fine inns and restaurants.

Toro Negro is an area of spectacular scenery and mountains. It has the island's tallest peaks and on clear days of which there are plenty, there are magnificent views of the Atlantic Ocean to the north and the Caribbean Sea to the south. The **Cerro de Punta** is 4389 feet (1338m) and the Toro Negro Forest Reserve also has the island's highest lake, El Guineo. North of Torro Negro is **Jayuya** where there are a number of artists studios, workshops and museums. **El Ceni Museum** on 144 has a fascinating exhibit of Indian artifacts. It is open Mon to Fri from 8.30am to 4.30pm and from 10am to 3pm at weekends. ☎ 828-1241. There are a number of Indian petroglyphs (rock carvings) in the area. From Jayuya return on 144 to 149 and head north.

Manatí stands at the junction with Highway 2 and the scenic Route 149 that runs through the central mountains to the south coast. The town's chief claim to fame is as the center of the island's main pineapple producing area. From Manatí head north to connect with the expressway for the drive back to San Juan passing **Vega Baja** to the north and **Vega Alta** to the south.

EATING OUT

Aibonito

La Piedra $-$$
Local, Route 7718
☎ 735-1034

Manatí

Su Casa $$
Local-Seafood, Route 670
☎ 884-0047 MG

Ponce

Canda's $$
Seafood/International
Alfonso X11 St
☎ 843-9223

El Ancia $$
Local-Seaffod, 9 Hostos
☎ 840-2450 MG

La Terraza $$-$$$
International. Ponce Hilton.
☎ 259-7676

Pito's $$
Seafood-Steaks, Route 2, Cucharas
☎ 841-4977 MG

Mark's $$
International, Hotel Meliá
☎ 841-4977

Salinas

Costa Marina $$
Carib/seafood. Road 701
☎ 824-6647

TOUR FOUR (250 MILES-400KM)

Take Expressway 22 or Highway 2 west from San Juan past the busy resort town of Dorado with its five golf courses and the world's longest swimming pool (1,776 ft-long) and then through Manatí to the historic town of **Arecibo**, founded in 1556. Arecibo is home of the Fun Valley

Park, the only theme amusement park on the island. It is open Wed to Mon from 10am to 10pm. ☎ 817-0415. A new attraction in the area is the Paseadora de la Boca, a 20-minute historical boat trip in the mouth of the Manatí River. To the east of the town is the **Cambalache Forest**, noted for its stands of teak, mahoe and eucalyptus trees, camping and hiking trails, while to the south in the **Río Abajo Forest** are classic karst landscapes, formed by water erosion on the porous limestone rock. Caving trips are available along the Tanama River that disappears underground.

Continue through **Hatillo** and **Camuy**. The stretch of coastline from **Quebradillas** round the coast to Aguadilla boasts one beautiful beach after another - all golden sand and fringed with palms. There are spectacular views of the Atlantic Ocean from suitably sited look-out points along the road. Inland is **Guajataca forest** with many well-marked trails through classic karst woodland landscape.

Isabela on Route 113 is famous as a centre for 'mundillo' or bobbin lace, Paso Fino horses and cock fighting. Take Route 459 west from Isabela then 467 for **Punta Borinquen**, which has excellent beaches and also boasts the longest airstrip in the Caribbean, part of the former Ramey Air Force Base. The golf course, formerly part of the military base, has been played by a number of US Presidents. Since the area was de-militarized, it has become a popular tourist spot because of its spectacular beaches. Nearby on road 458 north of Aguadilla is **Crash Boat** that gets its name because rescue launches were kept here in case of a plane crashing

into the sea. The waters off **Punta Borinquen** and **Crash Boat** both offer excellent snorkeling, and during the winter, when the surf tends to be better, the area is popular with surfers. Other good surfing beaches are **Gas Chambers** and **Wilderness**.

To the south Aguadilla looks out over the sweeping bay from its cliff top location. Although it is disputed, many historians believe that Columbus landed in the bay during his second voyage of discovery. The fresh water spring in El Parterre Park is where Columbus's men are said to have filled up their barrels of drinking water. The multi-colored fishing boats are pulled up high onto the beach, and you can visit the **Parque Colón** (Columbus Park). About 13 miles (21km) offshore is the small, unpopulated island of **Desecheo**. It is a great dive site and is really beautiful.

Continue south along the coast across the bridge over the river Culebrinas to **Aguada**, a Spanish settlement that was founded in 1510. There is another Columbus Park with monument, and public beach to the west, the **Balneario Pico de Piedra**, has lots of facilities and is popular.

Worth seeing are the church of **San Francisco de Asis** with its twin 100 foot towers in Paz Street, and the local museum housed in the old railway station. It is open Monday to Friday from 8am to noon. ☎ 868-6300. Call to arrange a visit.

Head south on 115 to Aguada and then continue past overhanging mango trees to visit the charming coastal town of Rincón, which nestles in the foothills of the La Cadena Mountains. The reef-lined beaches – **Antonio's Domes, Maria's** and **Tres Palmas** - have become popular winter haunts for surfers, while they are popular year-round with sunbathers and swimmers. The town is also home to many fine restaurants including the excellent **Horned Dorset Primavera Hotel**, which boasts one of the finest restaurants on the island, and has a number of nearby beaches. Among those to the north of the point, **Punta Higüero** faces the Atlantic Ocean and is popular with experienced surfers. The reef-lined beaches have been the venue for the World Surfing Championship on a number of occasions, and it was first held here in 1968. The beaches south of the point face the Caribbean, and the **La Cadena Mountains** act as a backdrop to both the beaches and the town. Rincón is a charming, quiet town with a nice yesteryear atmosphere.

The restored lighthouse at **Punta Higüero**, north of town, is in the center of an observation park from which you can whale-spot during the winter, as endangered humpback whales often gather here. From the point you can also see where the Atlantic and Caribbean meet, with a clear dividing line between the dark blue of the colder Atlantic and the warm waters of the Caribbean. Also nearby is the rusting dome of the former Nuclear Energy Plant. To the south and inland is Añasco. The land along the Añasco River is very fertile and is covered in huge sugar cane estates. The town itself serves the popular resort area with its sweeping bay and many public beaches. Nearby is the picturesque fishing community of Tres Hermanos.

From Añasco head north on Route 402R and 110 to Moca, famous as a center for the exquisite mundillo-style lace. The **Mundillo Lace Festival** is held here every June. **The Hacienda Enriqueta** on route 2 houses the town's museum. Palaceta Los Moureau on route 464 is an historic French provincial-style mansion. It is open Monday to Friday from 7.30am to 3.30pm. ☎ 877-3390. Also worth seeing are the **Colazzo waterfall** on route 111 east of town; **El Barandillo Bridge**, a swinging walking bridge over the Rio Guatemala on 446 close to town; and the beautiful **Lake Guajataca** on 119.

THE CAMUY CAVES

Take 111 east to San Sebastián and on to Lares to visit the spectacular caves. **The Camuy Caves** are in the Río Camuy Cave Park, which opened in December 1986. The 300-acre (120 hectare) park, on Route 129, 5 miles north of Lares, is one of the island's major tourist attractions, and rightly so. The vast cave complex is one of the world's most spectacular natural underground networks while **Río Camuy** is the world's third largest subterranean river. For the last four million years or so, the Río Camuy, has slowly been carving its way underground. The cave complex is so huge that it has still not been fully explored.

TRES PUEBLOS

The massive **Tres Pueblos Sinkhole** entrance, opened in October 1989, leads to one of the most impressive of the system's caves. It is 65 feet (20m) in diameter and 400 feet (122m) deep. There is some evidence that Taíno Indians lived in the sinkhole centuries before Columbus discovered the island

At Tres Pueblos, you can walk

along two platforms, one on the Lares side of town facing the houses of Camuy, and the other on the Hatillo side overlooking the massive cave and the River Camuy. For those with a head for heights, one of the platforms is suspended over the sinkhole with the river 400 feet (122m) below your feet in its fern-filled ravine. The sinkhole that is so large that it could accommodate the whole of the El Morro fortress. Tres Pueblos, on the boundaries of the Camuy, Hatillo and Lares municipalities, is one of many sinkholes in the Río Camuy cave system. Cueva Clara de Empalme opened in December 1986 and has been a major attraction ever since. There are 250 steps down to the entrance of the **Espiral sinkhole**.

Although the caves have only relatively recently opened to the public, they were discovered hundreds of years ago by Taíno Indians and more recently were used by locals for shelter and storage. The first scientific exploration of the cave system took place in 1958 and local boys who, like previous generations, had used the caves as a playground led the team to the site. Russell Gurnee, his wife Jeanne, José Limeres, a doctor from Puerto Rico who had explored the caves of San Germán as a boy, and Bob and Dorothy Reville, carried out the exploration. It was largely at the Gurnee's suggestion, that the Government purchased the land in order to establish the site as a natural preserve. In 1976, a team from the Speleological Society of Puerto Rico, under the direction of José A. Martínez-Oquendo, recommended the development of the **Empalme Cave**. The Society had thoroughly explored and mapped

the cave, and then went on to study and map others throughout the island.

The Government's purchase of the land allowed the ecological balance of the cave system to be maintained, and also offered visitors the opportunity of visiting this outstanding natural spectacle in safety and comfort. The exhibition and visitors' center of glass and local field stone and wood, has a reception area, café and theater, where there is an excellent audio-visual presentation describing the entire cave system, which can then be visited.

There are trolley buses to ferry visitors from the center to the Empalme and Tres Pueblos Sinkholes, and the mouth of **Cueva Clara**, where well-maintained footpaths wind through the 170 foot (52m) high cave. Guided tours of the caves usually last for about 45 minutes, and there are walkways through the caves providing easy access for all. The caves have enormous stalactite and stalagmite formations, and the area is packed with canyons, caverns and sinkholes. Apart from the tours of the caves, there are picnic areas, walking trails, food facilities and a gift shop. The caves are open 8am to 4pm from Wednesday to Sunday and on holidays. The last tour is at 3.50pm Cathedral Cave is the most recently opened section of cave complex. It gets its name because of the vast size of the cave and the buttress and column-like formations. **Cathedral Cave Wild Advenure** offers tours of the cave ☎ 898-3100.

Arecibo Observatory

To the east is the Arecibo Observatory. It is in the hills over-looking Arecibo at the end of Route 625 (which runs off Route 635 which turns off the 129), and has the world's largest radar-radio telescope, which covers 20 acres (8 hectares), the equivalent in size to 13 American football fields. A 600-ton suspended platform hovers over the dish site set in a sinkhole 565 feet (172m) below. Astronomers from Cornell University and the National Science Foundation who study planets and distant galaxies by gathering radio waves from space man the observatory.

The Observatory is also the home base for SETI, the Search for Extraterrestrial Intelligence. The observatory is open for self-guided tours from 12pm to 4pm Wednesday to Friday, and from 9am to 4pm on Sunday ☎ 878-2612.

From the Observatory, head north on 625 then take 623 to Esperanza to pick up highway 10. Follow this south past the Rio Abajo Recreation Area to Utuado.

To the west on 111, you can visit **The Caguana Indian Ceremonial Ball Park** built by Taíno Indians about 800 years ago for both recreation and worship. Some of the stone monoliths are etched with petroglyphs, and they surround several of the ten ball courts which were used for a game which some historians believe was the forerunner to soccer. It is amazing how the cobbled walkways have survived the centuries. There is a small museum of history and archaeology and a gift shop ☎ 894-7324.

South of Utuado is the lovely mountain town of **Adjuntas**. It is easy to get to now that the newly extended highway 10 runs south from the north coast to Ponce. Worth visiting is the **Casa Pueblo** cultural center housed in an historic building and with a butterfly garden alongside. It is open daily from 8am to 4pm. ☎ 829-4842. There is a museum of culture and tourism on San Joaquin, open Monday to Friday from 8am to 4.30pm and on Saturday from 9.30am to 2pm. ☎ 829-3310. The surrounding area offers stunning views, waterfalls, hiking and many Indian petroglyphs.

From Utuado you can head north on highway 10 for Expressway 22 and San Juan or you can detour east on 111 past **Lake Caonillas** to join highway 140 which crosses the Rio Grande before connecting with the 144 that runs north to the hill town of Jayuya. The town, nestling in the valley, is surrounded by spectacular peaks and there are many traces of the former Taino inhabitation.

E A T I N G   O U T

Aguada

Colinas $$
Spanish-Seafood, Parador
JB Hidden Village
☎ 868-8686 MG

Aguadilla

Darío's Gourmet $$
Continental, Route 110
☎ 890-6143 MG

Tres Amigos $$
Local, Route 107
☎ 882-8000 MG

New Golden Crown $$
Chinese, La Cima Hotel
☎ 890-5077

Dorado

El Ladrillo $$
International,
334 Méndez Vigo
☎ 796-2120 MG

Hyatt Cerromar Hotel $$-$$$
International, Route 693
☎ 796-1234

La Terraza $$
Seafood-Steak,
off Route 693
☎ 796-1242 MG

Su Casa $$-$$$
Carib/Spanish,
Hyatt Dorado Beach Hotel
☎ 278-1653

Jewel of Dorado $$
Chinese, Marginal St,
off Route 693
☎ 796-4644

Hatillo

El Buen Café $-$$
Local-Seafood, Highway 2
☎ 898-3495 MG

Isabela

Ocean Front $$
Seafood, Route 4466
☎ 872-3339

Jayuya

El Dujo $$
Local-Seafood, Route 140
☎ 828-1143 MG

Lares

Criollo $$
Carib, Route 129
☎ 897-6463 MG

El Taino $$
Carib. Route 129
☎ 645-4591

Quebradillas Casabi $$
Local, Parador Guajataca
☎ 895-3070 MG

Parador Vistamar
Local-International,
Route 113
☎ 895-2065 MG

Rincón

Landing $$-$$$
American/seafood,
Road 413
☎ 823-3112

Lazy Parrot $$
Carib, Road 413
☎ 823-5654

Utuado

Doña Fela $$
Local-Seafood, Highway 10
☎ 894-2758

Jungle Jim's $$
Carib/Vegetarian,
La Casa Grande Hotel
☎ 894-3939

TOUR FIVE (175 MILES 280KM)

From Ponce take Highway 2 west to **Guayanilla** and then south on 116 to **Guánica**, a delightful town nestling around a quiet bay. You can sit and enjoy a drink in the central plaza or go for a stroll along the sea wall, or enjoy a swim from one of the two beaches, the **Manglillo Grande** and secluded **Playa Jaboncillo**.

Guánica Forest

Visit the **Guánica Forest**, one of Puerto Rico's 20 splendid unspoiled forest reserves. It has the richest bird population on the island, and has the added attraction that it borders a number of beautiful sandy beaches, including the historic bay where US troops landed in 1898 during the Spanish-American war. The forest vegetation of stunted trees, scrub and cacti hugs the hills and ravines, is one of the world's best examples of a tropical dry forest, and in 1981 was designated a **United Nations Biosphere Reserve**. It is home to 134 species of birds, and 700 species of plants and trees, and also boasts many ancient Guayacán (lignum vitae) trees, the oldest of which is reputed to be more than 1,000 years old. At the ranger station, you can pick up orientation material and trail brochures. West of Guayanilla is Yauco, famous for its coffee and the annual **National Coffee Harvest Festival**. There is a small museum of art and culture. It is open Monday to Friday from 8am to 4.30pm. ☎ 267-0350. The Lago Luchetti wildlife refuge offers great birdwatching, hiking, fishing and camping.

From Guánica go west on 116 past Ensenada to La Parguera, a small fishing village that has developed into a popular tourist destination in the last few years, with a number of hotel and guest rooms, restaurants and many attractions, including superb diving, such as the **Puerto Rican Wall** that drops more than 1,500 feet (500m) and where rare black coral grows. There are more than 50 good dive sites offshore.

PHOSPHORESCENT BAY

One of the greatest attractions is a visit to the town of Lajas and the phosphorescent or bioluminiscent bay. There are two such bays in Puerto Rico and only a handful elsewhere in the world. The bay is seen to best effect on a moonless night when the special luminescent plankton cast their beautiful blue glow across the sea. You can take a boat ride into the bay and the movement of the boat causes the plankton to move in phosphorescent patterns around you. Also of interest is the area just offshore known as the Canals, which are a cluster of mangrove cays rich in wildlife. You can boat through the channels between the islands.

From Parguera head inland on routes 304, 116 and 101 through Lajas to visit the charming little hill town of **San Germán** which is most famous for the **Porta Coeli Museum Church**, built in 1606 and the oldest church still intact in the US. It is open Wed to Sun from 8.30am to noon and 1pm to 4.30pm. ☎ 892-5845. The town boasts many fine old buildings and has retained much of its old colonial character, and it makes a delightful day out either from San Juan or Ponce. You can stroll through the picturesque, historic streets full of Spanish Colonial charm and architectural styles spanning three centuries. San Germán was the main town of the southwest during the colonial era, and the administrative, political and cultural heart of the region until the end of the 19th century. It still plays an important role in the region's culture today.

The town was founded in 1512 and named after **Germaine de Foix**, the second wife of King Ferdinand of Spain. Many of its earliest inhabitants were far from law abiding and earned their living from smuggling or piracy, attacking the ships that sailed off the nearby southern shore. Many of the town's residents today can trace their lineage back to these turbulent times. After the privateers, the town got another boost when the area became a center for the sugar cane industry and was surrounded by plantations. Wealthy owners built fine houses in the town that became known as **Ciudad de las Lomas**, or City of the Hills, and it attracted both artists and craftsmen.

There is a wealth of old buildings, some dating back to the beginning of the 17th century. Predominant architectural styles date from the Spanish Colonial era, especially around the mid-19th century, Criollo from the 1880s, neo-Classical from the first two decades of the 20th century, Art Deco from the 1930s, and the newly emergent International style of the 1960s.

Because of this breadth of architectural styles and the number of well preserved buildings, San Germán is the second Puerto Rican city to be included in the National Register of Historic Places – the

Above: **Bioluminescent Bay, Lajas: La Parguera**

Right: **Lajas, La Parguera**

other being Old San Juan. In February 1994, a 36-acre (14 hectare) area of the town containing almost 250 important properties, was added to the National Register. There is a lovely walk around the town starting from the new City Hall on Calle Luna. It is only a short stroll west along Calle Luna and then north on Calle Javilla, to reach the **Acosta y Forés House** at 70 Calle Dr. Santiago Veve. The house is considered one of the two most beautiful homes in all Puerto Rico, the other is also in San Germán in Calle Luna. It is a fabulous example of criollo architecture, dating from 1917 and featuring traditional wood construction. A major feature of the property is the floor to ceiling painted stenciled designs on every

wall in every room.

Opposite is a park that features a map of Puerto Rico showing all the towns that sprang from San Germán during the Colonial period, including Ponce, Mayagüez, Lajas and Cabo Rojo. The map includes the dates each town was founded and shows the unique seal adopted by each of the communities.

A little further west on Calle Dr. Santiago Veve is the **Paul Kindy House**, a very well preserved example of neo-classical architecture, and then it is only a short walk to Porta Coeli and the town's main attraction.

The church was originally built by Dominican friars in 1606 and is the oldest church in the New World. In 1878, the chapel was restored and opened for services and these were held until 1949. In 1939, the church was recognized as a national historical monument, but was badly damaged aften being struck by lightning in 1948. It was closed for worship the following year, and was not re-opened until 1982 following an impressive restoration project undertaken by the Institute of Puerto Rican Culture. The Church, whose name translated means 'Gateway to Heaven', has been restored to resemble a working chapel, and Mass is held there three times a year, and it also houses the **Museum of Religious Art**. The original palm wood ceiling with its brown ausubo beams has been beautifully restored, and the chapel contains treasures from around the world. There are choral books from Santo Domingo, a 17th century portrait of St. Nicholas de Bari, the French Santa Claus; a primitive carving of Jesus found in San Juan, and a number of 19th century Señora de la Monserrate Black Madonna and Child statues. The chapel is open from 9am to noon and 1pm to 4.30pm Tuesday to Sunday and admission is free ☎ 892-5845.

At the junction of Calle Luna and Calle Ramas is the **Juán Ortíz Perichi House**, at 94 Calle Luna, which shares with Acosta y Forés House, the title of one of Puerto Rico's two most beautiful homes. It was built in the 1920s and designed by Luis Pardo Fradera, and is a fine example of Puerto Rican ornamental architecture, featuring a multilevel design with curved balcony and pitched roofs.

To the north on Calle Ramas, across the street from Porta Coeli, is the town's most popular and most easily recognized house, the **Tomás Vivoni House** at number 38. It is named after the architect who designed and built it in 1913. It is in Queen Anne style with tower and gables, which have become key elements in the town's profile.

Next-door is the **Parque de Santo Domingo**, one of the town's two main plazas. It was originally used as a market, selling produce drawn from throughout the region, but it is now a delightful place, bordered with black iron and wooden park benches overlooking busts of many of the town's historic and prominent figures. The plaza is also home of the Old City Hall and the Farmacia Martín, a Spanish Colonial building converted to a pharmacy, which it still is.

Just to the west of **Parque de Santo Domingo** is **Plaza Maríano Quiñones**, the town's other main plaza, and home of the **San Germán de Auxerre Church**. The church, built in the 19th century, is in the center of the rectangular plaza, and is noted for its wooden vaulting featuring trompe l'oeil painting in blue and gray. The original ceiling pattern was restored in 1993.

There are lots of places in and around the plaza to enjoy a snack or lunch, and then you can head west for Calle Esperanza where at number 23 and close to the junction with Calle Luna, is the Pablo Soto House, designed by eminent San Germán architect Pedro Tomás Vivoni. It features a wide, concrete balcony, colored glass and cement columns and pedestals.

Next-door is the small Alfredo Ramírez de Arellano y Rosell Art Museum, which displays art and turn of the century furniture in frequently changing exhibitions. It is open from 10am to noon and

1pm to 3pm Wednesday to Sunday ☎ 892-8870.

Opposite is the **Oliva Peréz House**, another noted San Germán landmark. The tall all-white building contrasts with the lush greenery of the gardens, and is considered one of the town's most tropical homes.

The old center of town is in the northwestern corner of San Germán. The Rafael García Cabrera School used to be the Casa del Rey, the headquarters of the Spanish Army during Colonial times, and the nearby basketball court was the Plaza de Armas, or parade ground in the 1700s.

This area of town also houses the **Inter-American University** that was founded in 1912 as the Instituto Politécnico. It was the first higher education institute on the island to be accredited by the Middle States Association of Colleges in 1944, and changed its name in 1956.

From San German follow highway 101 south to the small but very popular resort town of **Boquerón**, and still a thriving fishing community. It has an attractive beach on a sweeping bay that is ideal for swimming and boating. The town is also known for its excellent oysters sold from street stands, and for its hats that are woven from strips of palm leaves. **The Boquerón Lagoon** attracts large numbers of birds. From here you can visit **Cabo Rojo Lighthouse** (a long way south of the busy fishing town of the same name), the most southwesterly point on the island. The lighthouse was built in 1882 to indicate where the Mona Passage and Caribbean meet. There are many tiny islands and reefs offshore, and the mile long **Cayo Ron Reef**. To the east of town, the road passes the marshes that

attract so many birds, especially during the migration season. **The Cabo Rojo Wildlife Refuge** is home to more than 170 species of birds. This southwest corner of the island is particularly arid because of the low rainfall but there are many beautiful beaches in the area. Route 301 goes south 3301 and the small fishing village of **El Combate**. From here until Aguila Point salt flats back the narrow sandy beach.

Return along the 301 to Las Arenas, turn right on 101and then head north on103 that parallels the western coast heading north.

The stretch of coast along this part of the Mona Channel is popular with holidaymakers, and noted for its seafood restaurants. You can also take a mini-boat trip to the **Isla de Ratones** (Mice Island). Just south of Joyuda with its popular public beaches and many fine seafood restaurants, you can drive to the pretty but isolated fishing village of Puerto Real.

MAYAGÜEZ

Mayagüez is Puerto Rico's third largest city, the largest on the west coast, and an important port. It was a Taíno settlement and still carries its Indian name meaning 'place of many waters'. Settled by the Spanish in the 18th century, it was almost completely destroyed by an earthquake in 1918. A statue of Christopher Columbus stands on a globe pedestal in the main Plaza Colon and the city is noted for its many historic buildings including the post office and Yagüez Theater (movie theater), waterfront district and nearby **Juan A. Rivero Zoo** where many of the animals live on islands in the landscaped gardens. The zoo is open from 8.30am to

A long way offshore in the Mona Passage lies Mona, a remote, uninhabited island famous for its colonies of sea birds. They crowd on the 200-foot (61m) high limestone cliffs that circle much of Mona, spectacular marine life and dazzling white beaches. The island, 55 miles (92km) to the west of Puerto Rico, teems with iguanas, is home to three species of endangered sea turtles, red footed boobies and countless sea birds, and thus earns its other name of 'the Galápagos of the Caribbean'. It can be reached by charter boat from Mayagüez.

The plateau atop the cliffs has dry forests and cacti, and offers spectacular views over the surrounding coral reefs. The island offers great snorkeling and birding, and there is a complex honeycomb of caves carved out by the sea that can be explored by experienced cavers.

Mona supports 417 plant and tree species, many of which are unique to the island, and 78 species that are rare or endangered. Twenty endangered animals have been spotted, including three different sea turtles that nest on Mona's beaches. The island also has about 100 species of birds, of which two are only found on Mona. In addition there are also the three feet (1m) long iguanas that are protected by law.

Although now uninhabited, pre-Columbian Taíno Indians lived there for hundreds of years and it was later used as a base by pirates, including Captain Kidd, who used the caves to hide their captured treasures. Then the caves provided employment for guano miners. Guano is formed when bat droppings mix with limestone on the cave floors to form a rich crop fertilizer. Columbus landed on Mona during his 1494 voyage, and Ponce de León camped in the island for several days in 1508, en route for Puerto Rico.

Mona is the most remote of Puerto Rico's islands, and has miles of secluded white sandy beaches fringed with palm trees. The island has been declared a Natural Reserve because of its unspoiled state and ecological uniqueness, and the surrounding waters are a designated US National Marine Sanctuary. The beautiful pristine coral reefs are some of the most extensive and well-developed in Puerto Rico waters, and include patch reefs, black coral, spoor and groove systems, underwater caverns, deep water sponges, fringing reefs and algal reefs. The rich marine life includes octopus, lobster, queen conch, rays, barracuda, snapper, jack, grunt, angelfish, trunkfish, filefish, butterflyfish, dolphin, parrotfish, tuna, flying fish and many more. The waters are warm and there is generally visibility between 150 and 200 feet (46m and 61m). There are eleven known shipwrecks around the island, including Spanish galleons, and five species of whale visit the island's offshore waters.

There are no hotels and no electricity, but camping overnight - $1 a night - is allowed if arranged in advance. Everything needed has to be carried in, including water, and all waste must be carried out. It is a great place for sports diving. Encantos Ecotours offer a four-day, three-night tour of Mona with travel to and from San Juan ☎ 272-7241. There are also some cabins available, but most visitors prefer to visit by boat on day trips. The boat trip is long and can be rough. For information about overnight stays, contact the Department of Natural Resources ☎ 722-1726/3724.

4pm Wednesday to Sunday ☎ 834-8110. You can also visit the **Tropical Agricultural Research Station** in a former plantation, where there is a self-guiding trail through the tropical gardens. The gardens, run by the US Department of Agriculture, has one of the world's largest collections of tropical and semi tropical plants, It is open weekdays from 7am to 4pm ☎ 831-3435. Across from the gardens is the **Parque de Los Próceres** with fountains and shaded paths. To the north of the city there are a number of tuna fish canneries, then take Route 105 inland for Maricao, on the western slopes of the mountain range. On the outskirts of town is the Maricao Fish Hatchery. **The Maricao Forest** to the south of the town is another forest preserve, and interesting because it contains some of the island's driest vegetation. There is a visitor's center and wonderful views of the coast to the west. There is also a trail to the summit of Monte Guilarte that is in the heart of coffee country.

Continue inland on Route 105, east to Indiera Rita and then go north on 128 and 134 to connect with the expressway and the short run back into San Juan.

EATING OUT

Cabo Rojo

Agua al Culllo $$-$$$
Carib/seafood, Parador
Bahia Salinas
☎ 254-1212

La Cascada $$
Seafood, Parador
Boquemar
☎ 851-2158 MG

El Bohío $$
Seafood, Route 102
☎ 851-2755

Parador Los Flamboyanes
$$ Carib, Road 102
☎ 255-3765

Perichi's $$
Seafood-Steak, Route 102
☎ 851-3131 MG

Tino's $$
Seafood, Route 102
☎ 851-2976 MG

Tony's $$
Local-Seafood, Route 102
☎ 851-2500

Guánica

La Concha $-$$
Local-Seafood,
Playa Santa
☎ 821-5522 MG

Guayanilla

Pichi's $$
International, Route 132
☎ 835-4140 MG

Lajas

Villa Parguera Parador $$
Local-International,
Route 304
☎ 899-7777 MG

Maricao

La Casona de Juanita $$
Local, Route 105
☎ 838-2550 MG

Mayagüez

Chilli's Grill $$
American, 975 Hortos Ave
☎ 834-0880

El Castillo $$
Carib/International.
Mayaguez Resort and
Casino
☎ 832-3030

San Germán

Del Mar $$
Steak/seafood, Carro St
☎ 264-2715.

TOUR SIX (130 MILES - 208KM)

This route takes in one of the most beautiful stretches of the Panoramic Route that runs for 165 miles (266km) from Mayagüez on the west coast to Yabucoa close to the southeast coast. The route really consists of a network of 40 roads that run through the Cordillera Central via many rural towns and settlements. Apart from the tropical scenery and panoramic views, the route also offers the chance to visit traditional communities and get a taste of the real Puerto Rico. Along the way you can stop at one of the many 'colmados' for refreshments. These shops combine general store, bar and village meeting place, and there are many side roads into the mountains which can also be explored. It is advisable, however, to have a good, large scale map if you plan to venture off the beaten track.

From Ponce take Highway 10 north to connect with scenic Route 143 at Alto de la Bandera. Turn right and drive past Cerro de Punta on your left. You can detour north on routes 140 and 149/144 to visit Jayuya with its strong Indian traditions, and it makes a good base for exploring the mountains.

Continue east on 143 to Barranquitas, another crowded little mountain town with the Catholic Church on the highest ground. It is most noted for its two mausoleums, to **Luis Muñoz Rivera** and his son, former Governor Luis Muñoz Marín, and the small Muñoz Rivera Library Museum, open Tuesday, Wednesday, Friday and weekends from 8am to noon and 1pm to 4.30pm ☎ 857-0230. **San Cristóbal**

Canyon is the deepest canyon on the island and also has the largest waterfall. Take 162 south of Barranquitas for the turn off to the canyon.

Return to Route 162 and head south, then take 14 to the hill town of **Aibonito** in the heart of a major poultry and flower-growing area. It used to be a popular summer retreat as the wealthy escaped from the coastal heat. Visit the Gothic-style **Church of San Jose**, a national historic monument and famous for its gold laminated altar. The Mirador Piedra Degetau is an observation tower on route 7718.

Take Highway 14 south to cut back south through the Central Mountain Range to Coamo where there is a small historical museum open Monday to Friday from 8am to 4.30pm. ☎ 825-1495. For the **Coamo Springs** head south out of town, then take 153 to Las Flores and then 546. Then return to 14 and head west to Juana Díaz. It is then only a short drive back to Ponce.

EATING OUT

Aibonito

La Piedra $$
Local, Scenic Route 7718
☎ 735-1034 MG

TRAVELERS TIPS

Essential Information

Arrival, Entry Requirements and Customs

Visitors arriving from outside the United States are required to fill in an immigration form that must be presented on arrival. The form requires you to say where you will be staying on the island, and if you plan to move around, put down the first hotel you will be staying at. The immigration form is in two parts, one of which is stamped and returned to you in your passport. You must retain this until departure when the slip is retrieved as you check in at the airport.

Visitors from the United States do not require a passport, but all other visitors need a valid passport for entry. Check with your travel agent or airline whether a visa is required.

You may also be asked to show that you have a return ticket before being admitted.

US citizens do not need to clear customs or immigration, but other citizens must. If traveling on business, a letter confirming this may prove helpful in speeding your way through customs, especially if traveling with samples.

Having cleared immigration, you will have to go through customs, and may be asked to open your luggage for inspection. If you have expensive cameras, jewelry etc. it is a good idea to travel with a photocopy of the purchase receipt.

On departure, the luggage of US-bound passengers must be inspected by the US Agriculture Department, as laws prohibit taking certain plants and fruits into the US.

Cruise passengers landing for day visits need no documentation.

ACCOMMODATION

Puerto Rico has a wide range of accommodations to suit all tastes and pockets, from top class hotels to delightful guesthouses, self-catering apartments and beach cottages. Many of the new hotel developments have been planned with great regard for the environment, and several have won eco-tourism awards for their skilful use of natural materials that blend harmoniously with their unspoiled surroundings.

If you want to eat out and explore quite a lot, it may pay to stay in a hotel offering part board, or one of the guest houses on the island, some of them converted plantation homes, and generally offering excellent value for money. Puerto Rico is a year-round destination but prices are highest during the high season that runs from mid-December to mid-April. Rates can drop by as much as half at other times of the year, so it pays to shop around. It is worth remembering, however, that many Puerto Ricans holiday at home and like to spend their summer holidays in the countryside, so hotels catering for them tend to have higher prices during the summer with their low season over the winter months.

Fact File

Paradores

There are 23 Paradores Puertorriqueños (Country Inns) throughout Puerto Rico. All are located in buildings of historic interest or at sites of exceptional scenic beauty. All are outside metropolitan San Juan, and they range from magnificent centuries-old buildings in the heart of the countryside to small properties in picturesque fishing villages. The parador system was introduced in 1973 and apart from their outstanding locations, they also offer excellent value for money, and are noted for their service and fine food. The Parador designation is awarded by the Puerto Rico Tourism Company and reviewed annually, and only properties meeting their very exacting standards are allowed to use the name and symbol. The paradores can be booked from the United States ☎ 1-800-443-0266. They include: Parador Casa Grande, in Utuado, a few minutes from the Caguana Indian Ceremonial Park. Parador Vistamar overlooks a wide sandy beach near Quebradillas in karst country with its curious landscape of mounds, sinkholes and caves. Parador El Guajataca, the first Parador, is on the northwest coast near Guajataca Forest Preserve. El Faro in Aquadilla on the northwest coast, near several of the island's best beaches. Parador Villa Antonio, is 20 minutes from Mayagüez Airport and close to some of the island's best surfing. Parador El Sol is in the heart of Mayagüez on the west coast. Parador Boquemar, Villas del Mar Hau, Bahia Salinas, Highway Inn and Perichi's are near magnificent white sandy beaches on the southwest coast. Parador Oasis is in San Germán, on of the island's oldest settlements, and close to the historic Porta Coeli Church.

Parador Villa Parguera is in the southwest fishing village of La Parguera that is also popular with water sports enthusiasts. Parador Posada Porlamar is also located in Parguera. Parador Baños de Coamo is close to North America's oldest thermal springs, once believed to be Ponce de León's 'fountain of youth'. Hacienda Juanita is another parador on an historic coffee plantation in Maricao. JB Hidden Village is another new parador in Aguada, close to the surfing beaches at Rincón, and nearby secluded swimming beaches. Hotel Joyuda Beach is at the beach in pretty Cabo Rojo. Hacienda Gripiñas is in Jayuya in the mountains. Others on the coast include Caribbean Paradise at Patillas, El Buen Café, Hatillo, La Cima, Aquadilla, Fajardo Inn and Palmas de Lucia, Yabucoa and Villa del Mar, Lajas.

Guest Houses

There are 24 guesthouses on the island ranging in size from seven to 25 rooms and offering a relaxed, friendly family atmosphere. Many are on or near the beach, and some have pools or sundecks, and serve meals. Rates range from $35-125 for a double room. There are also apartments, holiday villas and beach cottages available for rent offering you the privacy of your own accommodation and the flexibility to eat in or out.

Some terms: MAP stands for Modified American Plan i.e. breakfast and dinner included. EP or European Plan means bed only and no meals. CP is Continental Plan which is bed and breakfast, and AP for American Plan, means room and all meals. Prices quoted by hotels are for rooms, whether one or two people are sharing, and you may find it difficult to get a reduction if you are traveling alone, but have a go. Prices, unless clearly stated, do not usually include the 7% Government tax (9% for hotels with casinos) and 10% service charge. $ denotes inexpensive accommodation, $$ moderate, and $$$ deluxe.

An A-Z of accommodations

San Juan

Arcade Inn $
☎ 725-0668
A 19-room inn with kitchen facilities and restaurant close to the Condado beach. Breakfast and drinks are served on the delightful patio. Close to all amenities.

Atlantic Beach $$
☎ 721-6900
An imposing 37-room hotel on the Condado beach with a good restaurant. A member of the International Gay Travel Association.

Best Western Hotel Pierre $$
☎ 721-1200
A conveniently located 184-room hotel with restaurant, bar and pool, and close to all amenities. Good base for both business and holiday.

Canario By The Lagoon $$
☎ 722-5058
An elegant 40-room European-style bed and breakfast establishment, centrally located in Condado and close to the beach.

Canario Inn $-$$
☎ 722-3861
A lovely 25-room bed and breakfast inn in the heart of Condado and close to the beach and all amenities.

Caribe Hilton and Casino $$$
☎ 721-0303
Set in 17 acres (seven hectares) by the beach, five minutes from San Juan, totally refurbished, with 672 rooms and suites, 12,000 sq. foot casino, Player's Bar, La Patisserie and new Oriental Restaurant, three other restaurants and two pools, with diving, fishing, health club, sailing and tennis.

Condado Plaza Hotel and Casino $$$
☎ 721-1000
One of the three hotels on the fashionable strip that runs down to Borinquen Park at the beginning of Ocean Park. The 580-room hotel is five minutes from Old San Juan, and noted for the Tony Roma's Restaurant. There are other restaurants, bars, pools, casino, and health club, and facilities for diving, fishing, sailing, tennis and all manner of sports, both land and water-based.

El Prado $-$$
☎ 728-5925
A delightful 22-room inn close to the beach, restaurants, casinos and other attractions. Rooms have kitchen facilities, and there is a Spanish-style patio around the pool.

Embassy Suites Hotel and Casino on Isla Verde, features two-room suites with separate living/working area, mini-kitchen, private bedroom and free full breakfasts. There is also a business center, conference and banquet rooms, fitness center, pool, golf and casino.

Empress Oceanfront $$-$$$
☎ 791-3083
A charming 30-room hotel by the waterside on Isla Verde, and noted for its seafood terrace restaurant and nightly entertainment. It is by the beach and has its own pool.

ESJ Towers $$$
☎ 791-5151
The Towers has 450 air-conditioned studios and larger apartments with fully equipped kitchens by the beach. The lobby is especially interesting as it is more like an art gallery with contemporary works from around the world. The property has a restaurant, Olympic-size pool, and private fitness center.

Excelsior Hotel $$-$$$
☎ 721-7400
This 140-room hotel is in Miramar overlooking Condado Lagoon, and close to the beach and shops. Most rooms have full kitchenettes, and there is Augusto's restaurant and Café Miramar, pool, fitness center and free beach transport.

Howard Johnson Hotel $$-$$$
☎ 728-1300
Isla Verde. A full service hotel with rooms and suites, restaurant and bars and close to beaches and all amenities.

Gallery Inn $$-$$$
☎ 722-1808
A charming property with 22 rooms and suites in an historic building owned by artist Jan D'Esopp and her husband Manuko Gandia. Lots of art for sale.

Inter-Continental San Juan $$$
☎ 791-6100 6100
This 415 beachfront hotel is in Isla Verde, five minutes from the airport, and set in beautiful tropical gardens. It has six noted restaurants, including the Momoyama (Japanese) and Ruth's Chris Steak House. It also offers nightly entertainment, massive casino, huge pool and swim up bar, and full water sports.

Mario's Hotel and Restaurant $
☎ 791-6868
The comfortable 59-room hotel offers good value for money, and is known for its several restaurants that offer local, seafood, Greek and Italian dishes. It also has a cocktail lounge, nightly entertainment.

Normandie $$$
☎ 729-2929
The magnificent hotel, built in 1939, is considered one of the finest examples of Art Deco architecture. Most rooms have parlor, working area and sunroom. There is a choice of restaurants, pool, business floor and conference facilities, with facilities for diving, sailing and water sports.

Playa $
☎ 791-1115
A small, 15-room ocean-side hotel on Isla Verde, with popular La Playita restaurant and bar, and close to all amenities.

Radisson Ambassador Plaza Hotel and Casino $$$
☎ 721-7300
This recently renovated first-class 233-room and suite resort is in the heart of the lively Condado area, ten minutes from Old San Juan and only half a block from the beach. It has three restaurants, three bars, pool, jacuzzi and health club, and state-of-the-art casino.

Regency Hotel $$-$$$
☎ 72210505
A 127-room beachfront hotel with freshwater pool overlooking the ocean and whirlpool. Rooms have some kitchen facilities, and there is a good restaurant and piano lounge, as well as banquet and meeting rooms. Guests are also able to use the facilities at the Condado Plaza Hotel and Casino.

Ritz Carlton San Juan Hotel and Casino $$$
☎ 253-1700
Luxury suites with gourmet restaurants, spa and fitness center, tennis, watersports and casino.

San Juan Marriott Hotel and Casino $$$
☎ 722-7000
An impressive luxury 525-room and suite beachfront hotel with restaurants, bars, casino and entertainment, plus a full range of water sports.

Toro $
☎ 725-5150
A value for money 50-room hotel in Miramar offering friendly, comfortable service. Rooms have kitchenettes and there is a restaurant.

Tres Palmas Inn $-$$
☎ 727-4617
A delightful 12-room beachside guesthouse offering comfort and value for money. It has pool and sun deck and a gourmet menu is available. It is close to all amenities.

Wyndham El San Juan Hotel and Casino $$$
☎ 791-1000
A luxury newly refurbished 392-room and suite beachfront hotel with five-award winning restaurants, pools, casino, nightly live entertainment, fitness center, sports program and offering diving, fishing, sailing, tennis and water sports. It is the only hotel in the Caribbean to be a member of Leading Hotels of the World.

Old San Juan

Hotel El Convento $$-$$$
☎ 723-9020
This historic building, which dates back to the 17th century, has been completely refurbished with 53 rooms and suites on the top three floors, with pool, sun deck and jacuzzi, and the first two floors hosting shops and entertainment center with music and dancing, and street level restaurants, bars and shops.

Hotel El Milano $$-$$$
☎ 729-9050
307 Fortaleza Ave
A beautifully restored 19th century 30 room hotel in the heart of the old city. It has a restaurant on the top floor offering great views.

Wyndham Old San Juan Hotel and Casino $$$
☎ 721-5100
A 240 room luxury property with gourmet restaurants, bars and rooftop pool as well as casino.

Adjuntas

Monte Río Hotel $
☎ 829-3705
The 23-room hotel is close to the central square of this mountain town, and is noted for its fine restaurant and friendly bar.

Aguada

JB Hidden Village Parador $-$$
☎ 868-8686
This delightful parador offers 25 luxury units with a noted restaurant that specializes in local dishes and seafood. There is a large pool and conference facilities.

Aguadilla

Parador La Cima $
☎ 890-2016
The hotel with 40 rooms is close to six secluded beaches and has a restaurant specializing in Mexican, Chinese and Continental cuisine. There is a bar and local facilities include pool, surfing, swimming, sailing tennis, golf, fitness center and riding.

Hacienda El Pedregal $
☎ 891-6068
This elegant 27-room hotel has restaurant, bar and pool, and is close to the Ramey Golf Course. Honeymoon packages and car rental are available.

Parador El Faro $
☎ 882-8000
The 50-room parador makes a good touring base and has restaurant, bar, pool, playground and conference facilities.

Fact File

Cabo Rojo

Boquemar Parador $
☎ 851-2158
This 63-room parador is noted for its Cascada restaurant which specialises in sea food, and the beautiful sunsets. It also offers bar, pools, water sports and fishing, and conference facilities.

Perichi's Parador $
☎ 851-3131
The 30 rooms overlook the beach, and the award-winning restaurant is noted for its local and international cuisine. Facilities include bar, diving, fishing, nearby golf, pool, sailing, tennis and windsurfing. It is also close to the airport and marina.

Caguas

Hampton Inn $$
A brand new 125-room hotel with restaurant, meeting and banqueting facilities.

Ceiba

Ceiba Country Inn $
☎ 885-0471
A delightful nine-room inn set in the hills with ocean views. Continental breakfast is served and there is a lounge and full facilities are offered at nearby Puerto Del Rey Marina.

Coamo

Baños de Coamo Parador $
☎ 825-2239
A beautifully-renovated 48-room hotel with good restaurant serving local and continental dishes. There is pool, poolside bar, tennis and the oldest hot thermal baths in the Americas. According to legend, the springs are the fountain of eternal youth that Ponce de León sought.

Culebra

Casa Bonita $$
☎ 794-2332
A new 92-room hotel specializing in watersports, scuba and sailing. Restaurant, café, bar, pool and dinghy dock.

Dorado

Embassy Suites Beach and Golf Resort $$-$$$
☎ 796-6125
A new property with 174 suites and 55 two-room apartments on the ocean.

Hyatt Dorado Beach $$$
☎ 796-1234
The 298-room hotel was designed by Laurance Rockefeller in 1954 and has recently been restored to its full, original splendor. It is 22 miles (35km) west of San Juan, and shares a 1,000 acres (400 hectares) complex with its sister hotel the Hyatt Regency Cerromar Beach. It offers casino, golf, health club, pools, sailing, water sports, tennis and windsurfing.

Hyatt Regency Cerromar Beach $$$
☎ 796-1234
The 504-room hotel, set in 1,000 acres (400 hectares) of beautiful tropical gardens, boasts the longest swimming pool in the world which includes 14 waterfalls, whirlpool and swim up bar. It offers golf, all weather tennis courts, diving, fishing, sailing, water sports, health club and spa, sports bar and casino.

Fajardo

Inter-Continental Cayo Largo $$$
☎ 801-5000
Set in 880 beachfront acres, the first phase of this development features 314 rooms, five restaurants, bars, huge spa, tennis, golf, marina and watersports. The main building, The Great House has 93 rooms, restaurants, cigar bar, conference room and ballroom. An additional 221 rooms are being added on the property.

Parador Fajardo Inn $

☎ 860-6000
A delightful ten-room hilltop inn set in five acres (two hectares) of tropical gardens.

Wyndham El Conquistador Resort and Country Club $$$

☎ 863-1000
This massive self-contained complex, 45 minutes from San Juan, boasts 926 rooms, 70 luxury one, two and three bedroom villas, 16 restaurants and lounges, casino, and for many years had the largest ballroom in the Caribbean (until the Westin Río Mar). The resort nestles atop a 300-foot (91m) cliff that separates the Atlantic Ocean and the Caribbean. Guest rooms are located in five distinct environments, from a colonial village to the exclusive Club El Conquistador, and the waterside Marine Village and harbor. There are pools, health club, tennis, two golf courses, diving, fishing, sailing and water sports from the resort's 55-slip marina, and a half hourly shuttle to the resort's exclusive beach on nearby Palomino Island. There is even a funicular (cable lift) to carry guests from the cliff top to the water's edge.

Guánica

Copamarina Beach Resort $$

☎ 821-0505
A 72-room hotel set on its own private beach with restaurant, diving, fishing, pool, sailing, tennis and submarine gardens, as well as conference facilities.

Humacao

Candelero Resort at Palmas del Mar $$$

☎ 852-6000
Set in 2,750 acres (1100 hectares) of beautifully landscaped tropical gardens, this ever-expanding luxury 450-room resort features two hotels and rental villas set along 3.5 miles (5km) of beach. The resort also has its own equestrian centre, and the largest tennis complex in the Caribbean with 20 courts, eight of them floodlit, and tennis pros. Coral Head Divers is the only full-service, on-site dive operation in Puerto Rico. There is a wealth of water sports, fishing and sailing from the Palmas del Mar's marina.It features a choice of restaurants, bars, disco, casino, fitness center, Gary Player-designed championship golf course, club house, children's program, shops and conference facilities.

Isabela

Costa Dorada Beach Resort $$

☎ 872-7255
A 52-room and suite resort set on a two mile (3.2km) unspoiled beach, with two restaurants, bar and cocktail lounge with live music, pools, diving, fishing, water sports, tennis, basketball, volleyball, gift shop and convention facilities.

Villa Montana $$

☎ 872-9554
More than 50 one to three bedroom villas set in 30 beachfront acres with al fresco dining and water sports.

Jayuya

Hacienda Gripiñas Parador $

☎ 828-1717
This historic 19-room parador is set in lovely gardens in the hills. It makes a good touring base and a place for peace and quiet. It has a restaurant and pool.

Lajas

Parador Villa del Mar $$-$$$

☎ 899-4265
A lovely 25 room property perched on top of the mountains with spectacular views. It has a restaurant and large pool.

Las Marías

Gutiérrez $
☎ 827-3100
A 13-room hilltop villa close to town and set in floral gardens. There are kitchen facilities, pool and meeting room.

Maricao

Parador Hacienda Juanita $
☎ 838-2551
A 21-room inn amid a traditional coffee plantation and noted for its restaurant and Criollo cuisine, and tropical gardens. It offers bar, tennis volleyball, handball, basketball, game room, gift shop and walking trails.

Mayagüez

Embajador Hotel $
☎ 833-3340
A 21-room comfortable hotel close to the city center with restaurant and pool, and close to all the sights. It offers continental breakfast and welcome drink.

Mayagüez Resort and Casino $$-$$$
☎ 832-3030
A luxury 141-room hilltop resort, 30 minutes by air or a three-hour leisurely drive from San Juan. Set in 20 acres (8 hectares) of landscaped gardens, it has restaurants, bar, tennis, casino, health club, pool and nearby diving, sailing, fishing, windsurfing and golf.

Patillas

Villa del Carmen Resort $-$$
☎ 839-7536
The 12 apartments and studios are on the beach set among palm trees and tropical gardens. Units have kitchens and there is diving, fishing, health club, pools and sailing. Restaurants and shops are in nearby Patillas.

Ponce

Holiday Inn $$-$$$
☎ 844-1200
A 120-room hotel and casino complex set around a large pool and tropical gardens, overlooking Ponce. It has a restaurant and is convenient for both business travelers and holidaymakers.

Meliá Hotel $
☎ 842-0260
An elegant 80-room hotel in the heart of historic Ponce, noted for its comfort and friendly service. The restaurant offers local and international cuisine. Continental breakfast is provided.

Ponce Hilton and Casino $$$
☎ 259-7676
The 156-room and suite hotel is set in 80 acres (32 hectares) along the Caribbean, and offers three restaurants, floodlit tennis courts, pool, new 18-hole golf course and conference facilities. There is also a health club, diving, fishing, and water sports.

Quebradillas

Vistamar Parador $-$$
☎ 895-2065
A 55-unit hilltop hotel with spectacular views. The restaurant overlooks the Atlantic. It has bar, live music at weekends, pool, tennis and conference facilities.

Rincón

The Horned Dorset Primavera Hotel $$$
☎ 823-4030
A luxurious, elegant property with 22 secluded suites complete with mahogany poster beds and other antiques. The magnificent Spanish Colonial building is set in equally magnificent grounds with a large freshwater pool. The hotel's restaurant is one of the best on the island. It is not a place for those who want lots to do, there is no TV and no children under 12 are allowed. Honeymoon packages are available (and considered by many to be the best)

Rio Grande

Westin Rio Mar Beach Resort $$-$$$
☎ 888-6000
The first all-inclusive resort in Rio Grande with luxury accommodation including one, two and three bedroom villas along one mile of beach. It has restaurants, bars, pools, two champion golf courses, tennis, spa, water sports and meeting facilities.

Salinas

Marina de Salinas $-$$
☎ 824-3185
The 33-unit hotel is next to the marina and offers restaurant, snack bar, bar, pool, shopping plaza, diving, fishing, water sports, sailing and extensive sailing services. There are also free boat trips to nearby islands.

San Germán

Hotel Oasis $
☎ 892-1175
A 52-room hotel close to the town center with good restaurant, bar, pool and convention center.

Utuado

Casa Grande Parador $
☎ 894-3939
Great value 20-room hillside property in its own private valley with pool and superb tropical scenery. It has a noted restaurant.

Vieques

Casa Del Francés $$
☎ 741-3751
Close to Esperanza it has 19 rooms. A delightfully laid back hotel in a former plantation Great House, designated an historic landmark. It has a restaurant noted for its seafood, pool and is close to the beach.

Crow's Nest $
☎ 741-0033
An appropriately named property set atop rolling hills in five acres (two hectares) of wooded grounds and gardens, but only a short drive to town and the beaches. Each unit has light cooking facilities, and there is a good restaurant, pool and bar. Diving, riding and sightseeing trips can be arranged.

Hacienda Tamarindo $$-$$$
☎ 741-8525. An exquisite 16 room hilltop hotel with spectacular views, free American breakfast and honor bar.

AIRLINES/AIRPORTS

ACES
☎ 800-846-2237

Air Calypso
☎ 253-0020

Air Canada
☎ 1-800-776-3000

Air Caraibes
☎ 253-0933

Air France
☎ 800-237-2747

Air Jamaica
☎ 800-523-5585

ALM
☎ 327-7230

American/American Eagle
☎ 749-1747

British Airways
☎ 1-800-247-9297/ 725-1575

BWIA
☎ 800-538-2942

COPA
☎ 722-6969

Delta
☎ 1-800-221-1212

Iberia
☎ 800-772-4642

Isla Nena
☎ 741-6362

LACSA
☎ 724-3444

LIAT
☎ 1-800-981-8585/791-0800

Lufthansa
800-645-3880

Northwest
☎ 800-253-0206

United
☎ 253-2776

USAir
☎ 1-800-842-5374

Vieques Air-Link
☎ 722-3736

BANKS

Banks are open Monday to Friday 8.30am to 4pm and some open on Saturdays from 10am to noon. Most major US banks have branches on the island. Automatic teller machines are widely available.

BEACHES/SWIMMING

Puerto Rico has more than 250 fabulous beaches, everything you ever dreamed of for a tropical island, miles of sand, a fringe of tall palms for shade, and turquoise clear warm seas. Balnearios, or public beaches have a modest admission charge but offer lockers, showers and cheap parking, but facilities are often not available on Mondays. It is also possible to camp overnight on or close to some beaches, and details can be obtained from ☎ 722-1551 or 721-2800.

Generally the best beaches are on the protected western coast although there are many fine, unspoiled beaches on the northern coast. Beaches on the windier Atlantic Ocean coast tend to have choppier seas but offer excellent surfing and windsurfing, and have fine sandy stretches.

Best beaches include: Añasco Beach on Route 401 near Añasco, Boquerón on Route 101, four miles (6km) from town, Caña Gorda on Route 333, four miles (6km) from Guánica, Piñones on Route 187, 2.4 miles (4km) from Isla Verde, Cerro Gordo on Route 690 at Vega Alta, Escambrón in Muñoz Rivera Avenue, Puerta de Tierra, Luquillo on Highway 3, 22 miles (35km) from Luquillo town, Punta Guilarte on Highway 3 east and west of Arroyo, Punta Salinas on Route 868 close to Cataño, Punta Santiago on Highway 3 east of Humacao, Sardinera on Route 698 at Dorado, Seven Seas on Route 987 at Fajardo, and Sombé (Sun Bay) on Route 997 at Vieques. Boquerón and El Combate in Cabo Rojo are considered by many to be the tops.

BUS

For Metrobus information ☎ 763-4141, and for Metropolitan Bus Authority services ☎ 250-6064. These only cover the San Juan metro area.

CAMPING

There are a number of campgrounds on the island and camping is allowed with permits on or close to many beaches. There are also campgrounds in many of the forest reserves. For further information contact the Forest Reserve ☎ 723-1718/724-3724, or the US Forest Service ☎ 766-5335/724-3647.

CAR RENTAL/DRIVING

Cars, mini vans and four-wheel-drive vehicles can be hired and provide the best way of exploring the island. If you plan to go at peak periods, it is best to hire your vehicle in advance through your travel agent. Cars can be hired, however, at airports, hotels or car hire offices on the island. Check the car thoroughly before accepting it, and make sure there is a jack and spare tire in good condition.

DRIVE ON THE RIGHT. The main roads are generally very good and highways and expressways help you get around the island quickly so most places can be explored as a day trip if you do not want to overnight away from your resort.

Car hire and driving rules

A valid driving license is needed if you want to hire a car in Puerto Rico, and you must be 21 years of age or over. Many overseas automobile clubs are affiliated with the American Automobile Association (AAA), and proof of membership of one of these, entitles you to a range of services, including breakdown assistance, free maps and discounts for car hire, hotels and many attractions.

Driving is a pleasure once you have got used to driving on the right hand side of the road and familiarized yourself with traffic signs and so on. Local drivers do drive fast, however, and close.

You must also be constantly on the look out for pot holes, especially on minor roads. In the mountains extra care is needed because of narrow, twisting roads, hairpin bends, and sometimes after heavy rain, landslides.

Accidents

If you are involved in any road accident, exchange particulars with other drivers and get the names and addresses of any witnesses. You must report to the police any accident that involves personal injury, or significant damage (anything other than a minor bump). Never admit liability, or say 'I'm sorry', which may be taken as an admission of responsibility. Some insurance companies will not honor a policy if a driver has admitted liability. If you are driving a rented car, notify the hire company as soon as possible. If people are injured, no matter how hard it seems, leave medical assistance to those who are qualified to administer it. If you try to help and something goes wrong, you could be sued for damages.

Car hire

It is usually cheaper to arrange your car hire through your travel company, or as part of a fly-drive package. Although it is optional, you are strongly advised to have collision damage waiver (CDW), and it is often cheaper to pre-pay this as well.

If flying in to San Juan, most of the major hire companies are situated on the airport or a short drive away. If off the airport, courtesy buses shuttle to and from the car pick-up point.

At the car hire check-in, hand over your driving license, proof that you are 21 or over (passport) and your pre-paid voucher if you have one. You will be asked for an address where you will be staying, and if you are touring, give the hotel or motel where you will be staying on the first night. If paying by voucher, you will also be asked for a credit card to pay for incidentals such as airport tax, additional drivers and so on.

When you check in, don't be persuaded to upgrade or take out unnecessary insurance. Be sure you understand what they are trying to sell you, and then decide if you need it. Cars available range from economy models to limousines, and some rental companies will urge you to upgrade because they have run out of vehicles in the category you ordered. If you upgrade, they will charge you for a bigger car, if you refuse, they will be obliged to give you a bigger car at their expense.

Driving under the influence of alcohol or drugs

Even having an open container of alcohol in a car is illegal, and it is just not worth the risk of drinking and driving. If convicted, the penalties are very severe, including imprisonment and vehicle confiscation. Driving under the influence of drugs is also a serious crime and you will probably end up in prison.

Emergencies — Breakdown

If your car breaks down in a rural area, move across on to the hard shoulder, lift the bonnet (hood), and then get back into the vehicle, lock the doors and wait for help. If it is at night, you must use your emergency flashers. Police cars cruise the highways and will come to your aid. If there is an emergency phone on the road, use that to call for assistance. If driving a rental car, notify the company as soon as possible so that a replacement can be provided.

Parking

When parking, choose a spot that is well lit and ideally, in a busy area. Lock all doors and make sure anything of value is out of sight.

Petrol (gas)

All cars now run on unleaded fuel, but getting fuel can be confusing as pumps operate in a number of different ways. Follow the instructions on the pump. Usually the nozzle has to be removed and then the bracket it rests on, moved into an upright position to activate the pump. Some filling stations require pre-payment, some accept credit cards that can be inserted into the pump that then gives a receipt, some stations will only accept cash, and others charge more for fuel paid for by credit card. Fuel is sold in liters.

Rules of the Road

- Always drive on the right and pass on the left.
- Buckle up because seat belts are compulsory.
- Observe speed limits: 65mph (112kph) on main highways, 55 mph (88 kph) on smaller roads, 30 mph (48km) in towns and 15 mph (24kph) in school zones. There are on the spot fines for speeding, and if you are caught going too fast, you could spend a night in jail. If stopped for speeding, don't pay the police officer, but pay fines direct to the relevant Clerk of the Court. Handing money to the policy officer might be misinterpreted as a bribe. The usual procedure is that the police impounds your driver's license, gives you a receipt, you have to go to the precinct where it was confiscated to retrieve the license, bringing with you a receipt from the Colecturía, or Treasury Department local office, certifying that you paid the fine. Then your license is handed back. If you delay more than a few days, the license goes to the regional police center.
- Report all traffic accidents to the local police within four hours.
- If a school bus stops with its flashers on, traffic in both directions must stop while children get on or off. Traffic can only move when the bus moves off. The only exception is when oncoming traffic is separated from the bus by a central reservation, in which case it can proceed.
- Do not park near a fire hydrant or in front of a bus stop. You will be fined and may be towed away.
- Never park in a handicapped-reserved space (they are marked in blue). The fine is very expensive.
- Always give way to emergency vehicles.

Fact File

- U-turns are legal unless there is a sign to the contrary.
- When it starts to rain, turn your headlights and wipers on and slow down.

Some useful signs:

area de cascanso	rest area
autopista	expressway
calle sin salida	dead end
carretera cerrada	road closed
ceda	yield
cruce de peatones	pedestrian crossing
cuidado	caution
despacio	slow
desprendimiento	landslide
desvío	detour
entrado	entrance
estación de peaje	toll booth
no entre	no entry
no estacione	no parking
pare	stop
peligro	danger
salida	exit
tránsito	one way
zona escolar	school zone

Hire companies (in San Juan unless specified) include:

AAA
☎ 791-1465

Afro
☎ 724-3720

Alamo
☎ 753-2265

Avis
☎ 253-5925/800-331-1084

Budget
☎ 791-0600

Charlie
☎ 728-2418

Discount
☎ 726-1460, 726-5930

Dollar
☎ 791-5500

Economy
☎ 784-0741

Hertz
☎ 791-0840

L&M
☎ 791-1160

Leaseway
☎ 791-5900

National
☎ 791-1805

Payless
☎ 832-0110

Popular (Mayagüez)
☎ 265-4848

Popular (Ponce)
☎ 259-4848

Target
☎ 782-6381

Thrifty
☎ 253-2525

Vías Car Rental
☎ 796-6404

CASINOS

There are many casinos on the island offering the full range of games of chance. The Ritz Carlton is the largest while others include the San Juan Grand Beach Hotel and Casino, Wyndham Old San Juan, Condado Plaza Hotel, Radisson Ambassador Plaza and Stellaris Casino at the San Juan Marriott Resort.

CHURCHES

Puerto Rico is predominantly Roman Catholic, but the island's constitution guarantees religious freedom, and after the United States' acquisition in 1898, a large protestant Pentecostal movement developed. Catholic services are held throughout the island in both Spanish and English. There is a Jewish Community Center in Miramar, and a Jewish Reform Congregation in Santurce. There are English-speaking Protestant services for Baptists, Episcopalians, Lutherans and Presbyterians, as well as inter-denominational services.

CLOTHING

Casual is the keyword but you can be as smart or as cool as you like. Beachwear is fine for the beach and pool areas, but cover up a little for the street. Informal is the order of the day and night, and this is not the place for suits and ties or evening gowns, unless you really like dressing up for dinner. During the day, light cotton, casual clothes are ideal for exploring in. During the evening, a light jumper may sometimes be needed. It is fun to change for dinner or the casino, but for men this normally means smart slacks or trousers, and for women a summer dress or similar. Dining out in San Juan can be more formal than elsewhere on the island.
If you plan to explore inland on foot, stout footwear and a good waterproof jacket are essential. Also, wear sunglasses and a hat to protect you from the sun during the hottest part of the day, and you will need sandals on the beach as the sand can get too hot to walk on.

CONFERENCES AND CONVENTIONS

Puerto Rico offers near-unrivalled conference and convention facilities. The new Puerto Rico Convention Center, covering 580,000 sq. feet is due to open in the fall of 2004. The San Juan-Puerto Rico Convention Bureau ☎ 725-2110 can answer most inquiries and assist with arrangements. Hotels offering major conference facilities include Caribe Hilton and Casino ☎ 721-0303, the Condado Trio - La Concha and El Centro ☎ 721-6090, and Condado Beach .Tel: 721-6090, Condado Plaza Hotel and Casino ☎ 721-1000, El Conquistador Resort and Country Club, Holiday Inn Crowne Plaza Hotel and Casino ☎ 253-2929, Hyatt Dorado Beach ☎ 796-1234, Hyatt Regency Cerromar Beach ☎ 796-1234, Mayagüez Hilton and

Casino ☎ 831-7575, Palmas Del Mar Resort ☎ 852-6000,
Ponce Hilton and Casino ☎ 259-7676, Radisson Ambassador Plaza
Hotel and Casino ☎ 721-7300, Radisson Normandie Hotel ☎ 729-
2929, Sands Hotel and Casino Beach Resort ☎ 791-6100, San Juan
Hotel and Casino ☎ 791-1000.

Consulates and embassies

Austria
Condado
☎ 766-0799

Germany
Río Piedras
☎ 771-9725

Mexico
Hato Rey
☎ 764-0258

Canada
Hato Rey
☎ 759-6629

Holland
Hato Rey
☎ 759-9400

Spain
Hato Rey
☎ 758-6090

Denmark
San Juan
☎ 725-2514

Italy
San Juan
☎ 767-5855

UK
Santurce
☎ 758-9828

France
Hato Rey
☎ 723-9662

Japan
San Juan
☎ 289-8725

CURRENCY

The official currency on the island is US dollar. The banks offer a
fixed, and generally a better rate of exchange than hotels and
shops. There are foreign exchange facilities in San Juan and at the
airport. Traveler checks, preferably in US dollars, are also accepted
in hotels and large stores, and all major credit cards can be used in
hotels, large stores and restaurants.

Note: Always have a few small denomination notes, either US$1
or US$5 notes for tips.

DEPARTURE TAX

The departure tax is included in the cost of the air ticket so there is
no need to save cash for this.

DISABLED FACILITIES

There are facilities for the disabled at most of the larger resorts and
attractions, and there are many sporting opportunities for the
handicapped. Facilities, however, vary enormously from good to
non-existent off the beaten track.

A special project at the Luquillo public beach - Mar Sin Barreras
(sea without barriers) occupies some 28,000 square meters of
prime oceanfront, with specially-designed bathrooms and showers,
six family-size gazebos, recreational areas and a ramp that leads to
two platforms inside the water. It can accommodate 65 handi-

capped bathers at a time and is open Mondays through Sundays from 8am to 4pm.

Other services for the handicapped available in Puerto Rico are provided by Wheelchair Getaways ☎ 726-4023, dedicated to renting specialized vehicles for wheelchair users, as well as meeting and greeting visitors at the airport and conducting tours of major attractions in Puerto Rico.

ELECTRICITY

The usual electricity supply is 120 volts AC 60 cycles. Adaptors are necessary for European appliances if they do not have dual voltage, and may be available at the hotel, or they can usually be purchased locally if you do not travel with your own.

EMERGENCY TELEPHONE NUMBERS

For Police, Fire and Ambulance dial 911.
Alternatives: Police ☎ 343-2020; Fire ☎ 343-2330

ENTERTAINMENT

Most of the hotels have some evening entertainment but this largely consists of live music over dinner.

ESSENTIAL THINGS TO PACK

Sun tan cream, sunglasses, sun hat, camera (and lots of film), insect repellant, binoculars if interested in bird watching and wildlife, and a small torch in case of power failures.

FERRIES

Ferries run between Old San Juan and Cataño every half hour each way between 6am and 9pm, and there are car and passenger ferry services from Fajardo to the islands of Vieques and Culebra.

FESTIVALS/PUBLIC HOLIDAYS *

January

New Year's Day (January 1) *

Three Kings Day – Epiphany – traditional gift-giving day

Puerto Rican International Folklore Festival

San Sebastián Street Festival

Eugenio María de Hostos Day

Martin Luther King's Birthday (January 16)

February

San Blas Marathon – really a half marathon in the hill town of Coamo

Arroyo's Cristobal Sánchez Festival

Coffee Harvest Festival – Maricao in the Cordillera Central Mountains

George Washington's Birthday (February 20)

Carnival – Ponce, San Germán, San Juan and Vega Alta

March

Abolición de la Esclavitud - Emancipation Day (March 22) - celebrating slaves' emancipation in 1873

Sugar Harvest Festival - San Germán

April

Palm Sunday (date varies)

Good Friday * (date varies)

Easter Sunday * (date varies)

José De Diego Day

Salinas Carnival

Maví Carnival

Patron Saint Festivals - Arecibo, Bayamón, Gurabo and Luquillo

May

Sabana Grande's Patron Saint Festival Day

Mother's Day

Ponce Danza Festival – a week of historical-cultural events. The Danza, similar to the waltz, was a popular dance at the turn of the century

Patron Saint Festivals – Camuy

Puerto Rico Heineken Jazzfest – a celebration of Latin jazz with international artists

Memorial Day

June

Patron Saint Festivals – Barranquitas, Carolina,Ceiba, Dorado, Guayama, Isabela, Maricao, Maunabo, Orocovis, Toa Alta, Toa Baja and Vieques

Tiroloco Tournament – the island's major national and international bowling event

San Juan Bautista Day

Casals Festival

July

Aibonito Flower Festival

Puerto Rico Bowling Federation's Annual Tournament

US Independence Day (July 4) *

Patron Saint Festivals – Arroyo, Cataño, and Morovis

Barranquitas Artisans' Fair

Luis Muñoz Rivera Day (July 19)

Loíza Carnival

Puerto Rican Constitution Day (July 25)

José Celso Barbosa's Birthday

August

September

Día del Trabajo – Labor Day (first Monday)

International Billfish Tournament.

October

Bomba y Plena Festival - a celebration of the island's Afro-Caribbean heritage.

Columbus Day - Día de la Raza

National Plantain Festival

November

Veteran's Day (November 11)

Puerto Rico International Film Festival

Jayuya Indian Festival – a celebration of the Taíno culture

Discovery Day (November 19)

Festival of Puerto Rican Music

Thanksgiving Day (date varies)

December

Bacardí Arts Festival

Lighting of the Town of Bethlehem, San Juan

Puerto Rico International Offshore Cup

Navidad – Christmas Day *

Hatillo Mask Festival, a Spanish tradition dating back to the town's founding in 1823

New Year's Eve

FISHING

Fishing is an island pursuit, and many islanders will fish for hours from harbor walls, from the beach or riverside. Deep sea and game fishing is mostly for blue marlin and tuna which can weigh more than 800lbs, wahoo and white marlin, which can weigh more than 100lbs and the fighting sailfish. Snapper, grouper, bonito, dorado and barracuda can all be kept close to shore. There are a number of boats available for charter or which offer deep-sea fishing.

FOREST RESERVES

The forest reserves are one of the great natural treasures of Puerto Rico, and have the added attraction of taking in wide-ranging habitats, from coastal plain to mountain. Most forests are accessible daily between 8am and 4pm, and camping is allowed in some with prior permission. For details call ☎ 723-1718, 724-3724 or 723-1770. The US Forest Service can be contacted on ☎ 766-5335 and 724-3647.

The forest reserves are: Aguirre Forest along the coast off Route 701 at Guayama; Boquerón Forest along the coast off Route 101 at Boquerón, Route 301 at Cabo Rojo and Route 304 at Lajas; Cambalache Forest on Route 682 at Arecibo; Carite Mountain Forest, off routes 184 and 179 near Guayama; Guajataca Forest on Route 466 near Isabela; Guánica Forest on the coast off routes 334, 325 and 333 near Guánica; Guilarte Mountain Forest off routes 518 and 131 at Adjuntas; Maricao Mountain Forest off Route 120 at Maricao; Piñones Coastal Forest off Route 187 near Carolina; Río Abajo Forest off Route 621 near Utuado; and the Toro Negro Mountain Forest off Route 143 at Jayuya.

HEALTH

Puerto Rico has the same high medical standards as found on the US mainland, and they are just as expensive, so comprehensive medical insurance is necessary as part of your holiday insurance. Most of the doctors are based in San Juan where there are 14 private hospitals, and most other areas are served by district hospitals. There are doctors in all major cities and towns.

There are no serious health problems although visitors should take precautions against the sun and mosquitoes, both of which can ruin your holiday. Immunization is not required unless traveling from an infected area within six days of arrival. All hotels have doctors either resident or on call.

The island has a specialty dive-medicine center and recompression chamber run by the US Navy at Roosevelt Roads, just south of Fajardo.

Tanning safely

The sun is very strong but sea breezes often disguise just how hot it is. If you are not used to the sun, take it carefully for the first two or three days, use a good sunscreen with a factor of 15 or higher, and do not sunbathe during the hottest parts of the day. Wear sunglasses and a sun hat. Sunglasses will protect you against the glare, especially strong on the beach, and sun hats will protect your head.

If you spend a lot of time swimming or scuba diving, take extra care, as you will burn even quicker because of the combination of salt water and sun.

Calamine lotion and preparations containing aloe are both useful in combating sunburn.

Irritating insects

Mosquitoes can be a problem although steps are taken by most hotels and resorts to minimize this. In your room, burn mosquito coils or use one of the many electrical plug in devices which burn an insect repelling tablet. Mosquitoes are not so much of a problem on or near the beaches because of onshore winds, but they may well bite you as you enjoy an openair evening meal. Use a good insect repellant, particularly if you are planning trips inland such as walking in the rainforests.

Lemon grass can be found growing naturally, and a handful of this in your room is also a useful mosquito deterrent.

Sand flies can be a problem on the beach. Despite their tiny size they can give you a nasty bite. And, ants abound, so make sure you check the ground carefully before sitting down, otherwise you might get bitten, and the bites can itch for days.

Note: Drinking water from the tap is safe, although bottled mineral and distilled water is widely available.

Air Ambulance
☎ 756-3424

Medical Emergencies
☎ 754-2222

HURRICANES

Puerto Rico is in the Caribbean hurricane belt but even though 1995 was one of the busiest hurricane seasons ever, all the major storms thankfully avoided the island.

Hurricane season is between August and early November, with September and early October the most likely month for these violent tropical storms, although most of these pass safely well north or south of the island. Weather stations track all tropical storms and give considerable warning of likely landfall. If a hurricane warning is issued, follow the advice given locally.

LANGUAGE

Both English and Spanish are official languages, although Spanish is the native language. English is widely spoken in San Juan and is taught throughout schools as a second language. Many English loan words are also now part of everyday Spanish.

LOST PROPERTY

Report lost property as soon as possible to your hotel or the nearest police station.

MEDIA

The San Juan Star is San Juan's daily English language newspaper. A free quarterly magazine, Qué Pasa, which gives details of attractions and things to do, is available in English. Many leading US and European papers and magazines are readily available.

MUSIC

Music is a way of life and the philosophy is often the louder it is played, the better. Cars, mini-van buses and open doorways all seem to blast music out, and once the music starts it goes on for hours.

NIGHTLIFE

If you really want to party, San Juan is a city that never seems to sleep. It offers the full spectrum of entertainment from opera and classical concerts to nightclubs and casinos, and traditional folk and dance companies. The Puerto Ricans are a naturally exuberant people and on Friday nights, they like to dress up and hit the nightspots. Hot spots include Babylon at the Wyndham El San Juan, Rumba in Old San Juan, The Water Club, Isla Verde, Martini's, San Juan Grand, El Chico Bar, Wyndhams El San Juan Hotel.

PERSONAL INSURANCE AND MEDICAL COVER

Make sure you have adequate personal insurance and medical cover. If you need to call out a doctor or have medical treatment, you will probably have to pay for it at the time, so keep all receipts so that you can reclaim on your insurance.

PETS

Dogs and cats can be brought into Puerto Rico from the US if accompanied by two documents: a health certificate dated not more

than 10 days before departure showing the animal is certified disease-free by a veterinarian, and a certificate of rabies vaccination, dated not more than 30 days before departure, and authenticated by the proper authorities.

PHOTOGRAPHY

The intensity of the sun can play havoc with your films, especially if photographing near water or white sand. Compensate for the brightness, otherwise your photographs will come out over-exposed and wishy-washy. The heat can actually damage film so store reels in a box or bag in the hotel fridge if there is one. Also remember to protect your camera if on the beach, as a single grain of sand is all it takes to jam your camera.

It is very easy to get 'click happy' in the Caribbean, but be tactful when taking photographs. Many islanders are shy or simply fed up with being photographed.

PORTS

The main port is San Juan that is also the cruise ship capital of the world. There are also major port facilities at Mayagüez and several marinas.

POST OFFICE

The General Post Office is just inland from the Cruise Ship Terminal in Old San Juan, and there are post offices in all towns and suburban areas.

PUBLIC TOILETS

There are not many public toilets on the island, but bars, restaurants and hotels have private facilities that can usually be used if you ask politely.

RESTAURANTS

There is a remarkably large choice when it comes to eating out on the island. San Juan has some of the finest restaurants in the Caribbean offering traditional regional cuisine, a subtle blend of Spanish, Creole and native Indian, and ethnic cooking from around the world.

There are the inevitable fast food burger, pizza and fried chicken outlets, beach cafés offering excellent value for the money, and elegant upmarket dining rooms, as well as restaurants offering the cuisines of Argentina, China, France, Italy, Mexico and many more. Many of the island's best restaurants are Mesones Gastronómicos (gastronomic inns) that are located outside San Juan. They feature local cuisine at affordable prices.

Most accept credit cards and during peak times of the year, reservations are recommended. If you come across a restaurant not listed in the guide, or have comments about any of those that are, I would very much like to hear from you.

The restaurants listed in the itineraries are classified by price –
$ inexpensive, $$ moderate, $$$ expensive.

SECURITY

It makes sense like anywhere else, not to walk around wearing expensive jewelry or flashing large sums of money.

Don't carry around your passport, traveler checks or all your money. Keep them secure in your room or in a hotel safety deposit box. It is also a good idea to have photocopies of the information page of your passport, your air ticket and holiday insurance policy. All will help greatly if the originals are lost.

As with most tourist destinations, you might be pestered by touts trying to sell tours, souvenirs and even drugs, or by young people begging. A firm 'no' or 'not interested', is normally enough to persuade them to try someone else.

SERVICE CHARGES AND TAXES

There is a Government hotel tax of 9% although 11% is levied if the hotel has a casino. Service charges are not usually added to restaurant bills, although they can be, so check before leaving a tip, which should be about 15%. In shops, the price on the label is generally what you pay but when buying in markets and from street vendors, you can try haggling over the price.

SHOPPING

One of the main advantages of shopping in Puerto Rico is that there is no sales tax, and for US visitors, no limit on what you spend because purchases are duty-free.

There is duty-free shopping at Luis Muñoz Marín International Airport, and a number of factory outlets in Old San Juan. Calle Del Cristo and Fortaleza are Old San Juan's main shopping streets. Top name clothing, jewelry, perfumes and electrical goods can be found, and there is a wide range of imported goods, from Thai silk to Spanish antique furniture and South American diamonds and emeralds.

Puerto Rico has world-class designers who incorporate traditional fashions and tastes into contemporary clothing. Best bargains include local designer clothes, jewelry and other accessories from the boutiques of Old San Juan, Condado and Isla Verde, and the main shopping malls across the island, including Plaza Las Américas in Hato Rey, the largest mall in the Caribbean, with more than 300 stores, 21 movie theaters and more than 30 restaurants and eateries.

Best 'local' buys include traditional santos – small religious figures hand-carved from wood by generations of local craftsmen. The best quality santos figures are real works of art and command high prices, and are highly collectible.

You can also buy ceramics, macramé, and handmade mundillo lace that originated in Spain. Masks also make good souvenirs. They feature heavily in island carnivals and celebrations and can be made from coconut fibers or papier-mâché. Cuatros - handmade, 10-stringed instruments somewhat resembling guitars, are also popular, and Ciales on Route 149, and Ceiba on Highway 3 on the east coast, are reputed to make the finest. There is also the excellent island rum and coffee, hand-rolled cigars, and island casual clothing.

And, it is thought the Taíno Indians created the hammock, and certainly Columbus took them back to Europe from where they spread around the world. You can still buy beautiful hammocks on the island.

Shops are usually open between 9am and 6pm Monday to Saturday and 11am to 5pm on Sunday.

SIGHTSEEING/TOURS

Sightseeing and island tours by land or sea can be organized through hotels, tour representatives or one of the many specialist tour companies on the island. Most of these are based in San Juan and include: **AAA Tours** ☎ 793-3688, **Acampo** ☎ 706-0695, **American Tours of Puerto Rico** ☎ 547-1819, **Atabeira Educational Travel** ☎ 767-4023, **Aventuras Tierra Adentro** ☎ 766-0470, **Caribbean Helicopr San Juan** ☎ 722-1984, **Copladet Nature and Adventure Travel** ☎ 765-8595, **Cordero Caribbean Tours** ☎ 786-9114, **Countryside Tours** ☎ 723-9691, **Encantos Ecotours** ☎ 272-0005, **Normandie Tours** ☎ 722-6308, **Oneida Star Line, Ponce** ☎ 840-8435, **Rico Suntours** ☎ 722-2080, **Sunshine Tours** ☎ 721-7300, **Tour Co-op of Puerto Rico** ☎ 253-1448/253-1606, **Tropix Wellness Tours** ☎ 268-2173, **Turismo Internacional** ☎ 721-1347, **United Tour Guides** ☎ 723-5578, and **Total Quality Tours** ☎ 720-5454.

SPORT

Unlike other Caribbean islands where cricket is king, baseball is the national sport in Puerto Rico. Fans follow the professional teams fervently, and during the off-season, amateur baseball takes over from October to February. Basketball is also very popular with amateurs and there is a new pro league. Historically, cockfighting has always been popular, especially in rural areas, and major tournaments are held every year in February, May and August.

Most hotels offer a variety of sports and water activities, and there are diving schools where you can learn what it is all about and progress to advanced level if you have the time.

Walking is great fun and there are lots of trails but have stout, non-slip footwear and a waterproof jacket. Protect yourself against insects, carry adequate drinking water and keep an eye on the time, because night falls quickly and you don't want to be caught out on the trail after dark. Guides can be arranged to escort you on these walks and make sure you get the most out of your trip.

Bowling

There are lanes at Tower Lane Bowling, Levitttown, Paradise Bowling in Puerto Nuevo, Cupey in Trujillo Alto, and Ponce Bowling in Ponce and Western Bowling in Mayagüez. Tower Lane Bowling hosts the week long Tiroloco International Bowling Tournament.

Cycling

There are scores of cycle clubs in Puerto Rico and cycling and road racing is hugely popular. Every year during the second week of May, riders from scores of clubs from both Puerto Rico and other Caribbean islands race against each other in the International Cycling Competition in Sabana Grande. The Tour Gigante de Puerto Rico also attracts a large field and larger crowds. Contact the Cycling Federation on ☎ 721-8755.

Fitness Gyms/Health Centres and Spas

There are gym and work out facilities at the Caribe Spa in the Caribe Hilton, which also offers aerobic and yoga classes, massages, herbal wraps, facials and loofah body polishes. The Plaza Spa at the Condado Plaza Hotel and Casino offers exercise machine and weight training, sauna, whirlpool, facials and massage. The Penthouse Spa at the El San Juan Hotel and Casino has fitness evaluations, supervised weight loss programs, aerobic classes, sauna, steam room and massage. The Spa Caribe at the Hyatt Regency Cerromar Beach has shape-up programs, aerobics, fitness machines, and skin and body care treatments including massage, facials and loofah polish.

The fitness center at the Palmas del Mar Resort in Humacao features hydra-fitness exercise equipment, free-weight training and computerized evaluations.

Fishing

The offshore waters offer world-class deep sea and game fishing, and catches have set more than 30 world records. Puerto Rico hosts many deep sea fishing tournaments which attract top class anglers from around the world, and the Annual Club Náutico International Billfish Tournament, held in September, is the world's largest and longest established tournament of its kind. Main deep water species include blue and white marlin, bonito, tuna, bonefish, tarpon, jack, kingfish, dolphin (dorado), sailfish, grouper and wahoo.

Deep sea fishing boats can be chartered in San Juan, Aguadilla, Fajardo, Humacao, Mayagüez, Parguera, Ponce and many other

towns and coastal villages. Aguadilla's new harbor opened in 1995 and offers excellent deep sea fishing along the Mona Passage.

Inland there is lake, river and mountain tarn fishing for largemouth bass, peacock bass, sunfish and catfish, and tilapia is also popular. Lake Dos Bocas in Utuado, between routes 10 and 140, and Lake Guajataca in Quebradillas, north of Route 111 offer good fishing. For more details about fishing and regulations, contact the Department of Natural Resources ☎ 722-5938

The following offer fishing trips and charters:
Benítez Fishing Charters, San Juan ☎ 723-2292
Caribbean Outfitters, Carolina ☎ 396-8346
Castillo Water sports, San Juan ☎ 791-6195
Great Lady Luxury Charters ☎ 796-1242
Mike Benitez Fishing Charters, Santurce ☎ 723-2292
Parguera Fishing Charters, Parguera ☎ 899-4698
Shiraz Fishing Charters, Palmas del Mar ☎ 285-5718
Tour Marine, Cabo Rojo ☎ 851-9259
Tropical Fishing Charters, Fajardo ☎ 266-4524

Golf

There are some 22 golf courses on the island, 12 of them championship courses that attract some of the world's top golfers. Both the Ladies PGA and Senior PGA Tours play their last rounds of the season on the island. There are public courses but most are part of major resort complexes, although non guests are welcome to play at all except at the Wyndham El Conquistador Resort and Country Club ☎ 863-6784. The Hyatt Regency Cerromar (796-8915) and Hyatt Dorado Beach Resorts ☎ 796-8961, each has two 18-hole courses, all designed by Robert Trent Jones. The Hyatt Dorado Beach was originally founded by Laurance Rockefeller. Each December, Dorado Beach hosts the Hyatt Senior Tour Championship in which the top 30 players on the PGA Senior tour compete for $1 million in prize money. The 6,985-yard (6389m) par-72 East Course at Dorado Beach includes the famous par 540 yard (494m) 13th hole. Because of its water challenges, both ponds and the Atlantic Ocean, the hole is ranked by Jack Nicklaus as one of the top ten holes in the world. The resort's West Course is 6,913 yards (6323m). The two courses at the Hyatt Regency Cerromar are not rated difficult, the South Course is 7,047 yards (6445m), and the North Course 6,841 yards (6257m).

There are the 72-par Ocean and River courses at the Westin Río Mar ☎ 888-6000 in Río Grande and the Palmas del Mar course .Tel: 285-2256 in Humacao. The former is challenging because of its narrow fairways and water traps, and was designed by George Fazio, while the latter is considered one of the island's finest links. The par-72, 6,690-yard (6119m) course was designed by Gary Player. The 11th to 15th holes are regarded as the toughest five consecutive holes in the Caribbean.

Set in 75 acres (30 hectares) east of San Juan the last three holes of the Bahía Beach Plantation course are played along the beach ☎ 256-5600. Dorado del Mar Country Club ☎ 796-3070, has an 18-hole course, and the Berwind Country Club ☎ 876-3056, near Río Grande, has an 18-hole 6,991 yard (6394m) palm-tree strewn course. The Punta Borinquen Golf Club ☎ 890-2987 is an 18-hole championship course at the former Ramey Air Base in Aguadilla in the northwest part of the island, and said to have been designed for General, later President Eisenhower. Greens fees and price of equipment rental vary from course to course according to the season ☎ 890-2987.

Other courses include the Coamo Springs Golf and Tennis Club with an 18-hole, 70 par 6,218 yard course ☎ 825-1370,; Palmas del Mar Country Club, with an 18 hole, 71 par, 6, 126 yard course, ☎ 285-2221; the nine-hole Aguirre Golf Club at Aguirre, the oldest course on the island which opened in 1926 on a sugar plantation ☎ 853-4052; and the nine-hole Club Deportivo del Oeste at Cabo Rojo ☎ 254-3748.The Wyndham El Conquistador Resort and Country Club in Fajardo has a beautiful 72-par 6,700-yard (6, 359m) course designed by Arthur Hills, but the course is only open to resort guests.

New courses have recently opened at the Cayo Largo Inter-Continental, Fajardo, and Hampton Inn in Caguas, while two 18-hole courses are due to open at Padadisus Puerto Rico Sol Melia in Rio Grande in 2003.

Hiking

There are many spectacular walks around the island, especially along the coast or through the Forest Reserves. You can explore mountain trails, mangrove swamps, moon-like karst landscapes, nature reserves, or sierra palm forests. Most of the paths are in good condition and well signposted. Some of the best walks are in the Caribbean National Forest, and include a number of leisurely trails up El Yunque, the taxing El Toro trail which really needs a full day, and the Mount Britton trail which needs an hour or so.

If you are planning to walk to remote interior locations it is advisable to hire a guide for the trip. Guides can be arranged at very reasonable cost, and they will ensure that you get the most out of your trip - and find your Away back. Puerto Rico offers great walking but the going can be tough not only because of the steepness of some of the terrain, but also because of the heat and humidity. It is essential to drink plenty of water and take frequent rests, as the walking may be more tiring than you realize. Luckily there are lots of waterfalls about which provide refreshment and a place to cool off.

Sensible, sturdy footwear is essential, and if you are a serious walker, a large-scale topographical map is essential, and can be obtained from either the park office or the Minillas Government Center in Santurce. Permits are required for wilderness travel so check first.

Horse Racing/Polo

There is racing from 2.30pm every Sunday, Wednesday and Friday – plus special holidays – at the El Comandante course on Highway 3 near Canóvanas, east of San Juan. It is a very modern track and attracts good thoroughbred fields. Off-track betting is legal and very popular in Puerto Rico.

Polo has achieved great popularity in recent years and is a very exciting spectator sport. The Ingenio Polo Club ☎ 752-8181, is close to Carolina, and you can watch the players practice as well as compete. The Club is the venue in March and August for the Audemars Piaget Polo Cup.

Horseback Riding

You can ride along the beaches or the many trails and riding instruction is available through **The Palmas del Mar Equestrian Center** ☎ 852-6000, **The Hacienda Carabalí** ☎ 889-5820, **Tropical Horseback Riding** ☎ 720-5454, **Tropical Trail Rides** ☎ 872-9256, **Hacienda Campo Alegre Yauco** ☎ 856-2609 and **Rancho de Caballos de Utuado** ☎ 894-0240.

Puerto Rico is world famous for its elegant Paso Fino breed of horses, considered by many as the smoothest riding horse in the world because of its unique gait. There are Paso Fino competitions throughout the island where riders and horses can show off their skills. Two of the most important Paso Fino events are the Dulce Sueño Fair in Guayama, held over the first weekend of March, and Festival La Candelaria, held during the first weekend of February in Manatí.

Marathons and Triathlons

Road running is also popular with many races and international events. The San Blas 20k Race is the major event of the year and takes place in February in Coamo, attracting a top field of international runners. The grueling Enrique Ramírez Marathon is held in April in Lajas and is a qualifying event for Puerto Rico's Olympic and Pan American Games hopefuls. The major women's marathon is held in Guayanilla in November, and the invitation race regularly attracts top women runners from around the world. Also held in November is the La Guadalupe 40-mile marathon held in Ponce.

Mountain Biking

Not for the faint hearted, but now offered by some tour operators.

Power Boating

Offshore power boating is very popular, and there are races throughout the year, especially off the west coast between Mayagüez and Boquerón. The main event of the racing calendar is the international Caribbean Offshore Race that always attracts a top field of the world's best, and huge crowds.

Scuba diving/snorkeling

The waters off Puerto Rico offer some of the best diving in the world. The waters are warm and generally clear, the reefs are easily accessible and they teem with marine life, and there is a wide choice of dive shops and operators, most PADI or NAUI certified. Visibility can be affected after heavy rains because of the volume of river water running into the sea, but having said that, average visibility is about 70 feet (21m), and can be much greater away from river mouths and other coastal water outlets. This fresh water run-off does have a major advantage, however, in that it attracts large numbers of fish not normally seen so close to shore. You might also spot the gentle giant manatee, or sea cow swimming close to the shore.

The best diving areas include:

Aguadilla and Rincón: with dives from 35 to 120 feet (12-40m), and especially off Desecheo Island 12 miles (19km) to the west, which is noted for its caves, rich fish life and giant sponges.
Cayo Icacos, Lobos and Palominos: all reached by boat from San Juan or Fajardo, offer boat and beach dives in up to 45 ft (15m) of water.
Culebra: which has reefs, wrecks, caves and walls in up to 90ft (30m) of water.
Dorado: offers diving to 30 feet (10m) from Dorado beaches. Crash Boat near Rincón .
Fajardo: offers deep dives up to 100 feet (30m) and trips to Culebra, Vieques and other islands.
Humacao: offers the chance to dive around Cayo Santiago.
Isabela: is popular for beach diving and the waters up to 60 feet (20m) deep cover extensive cave formations.
Mona Island: is difficult to get to but well worth the boat ride. The area is protected and unspoiled. Visibility is excellent and more than 300 species of fish have been recorded here. There is also excellent wall diving with caves to explore.
Parguera: is noted for its wall dives and the chance to dive in the phosphorescent waters and nearby mangrove canals.
Ponce: has good offshore reef diving. The barrier reef consists of a number of islands, including Caja de Muerto.
San Juan is great for beginners and there are a number of courses available. Training courses are held in hotel pools or from the beach close to the hotel, and there is good shore diving in up to 90 feet (30m) of water.
Vieques: offers wonderful diving from near deserted beaches with walls, caves and reefs to explore in 90 feet (30m) of water.

The following offer diving training, tours and water sports:

Adventure By The Sea
Toa Baja
☎ 374-1410

Aquatica Underwater Adventures
Aguadilla
☎ 890-6071

Calypso Divers
La Parguera
☎ 866-5816

Caribe Aquatic Adventure
San Juan
☎ 724-1882

Caribbean Divers Institute
Fajardo
☎ 860-2177

Caribbean School of Aquatics
San Juan
☎ 728-6606

Casa del Mar Dive Center
Fajardo
☎ 860-3483

Castillo Water sports
San Juan
☎ 791-6195

Coral Head Divers, Humacao
☎ 1-800-635-4529/850-7208

Coral Reef Divers, Cabo Rojo
☎ 255-3483

Culebra Dive Shop, Culebra
☎ 742-3555

Discover Scuba Diving, Fajardo
☎ 863-4300

Dive Copamarina
Guánica
☎ 821-0505

Dive Puerto Rico
Fajardo, Culebra and Vieques

Humacao Diver Service Center
Humacao
☎ 852-4530

Into The Blue Dive Travel Services
☎ 1-800-6-GETWET

Island Venture
Ponce
☎ 842-8546

Mundo Submarino
San Juan
☎ 791-5764

Paradise Scuba and Snorkeling Center
Lajas
☎ 899-7611

Parguera Divers
Parguera
☎ 899-4171

Palomino Divers
El Conquistador, Fajardo
☎ 863-1077

Scubo Centro
San Juan
☎ 781-8086

Scuba Connection
Caguas
☎ 744-8578

Sea Ventures
Fajardo
☎ 739-3483

Tennis

There are more than 100 tennis courts around the island, and 17 floodlit courts in San Juan's Central Park ☎ 722-1646. Hotels in San Juan with lit courts include: **Caribe Hilton and Casino** ☎ 721-0303, **Carib Inn** ☎ 791-3535, **Condado Plaza Hotel and Casino** ☎ 721-1000, and **El San Juan Hotel and Casino**. Elsewhere there are courts at the **Ponce Hilton** ☎ 259-7676, **Copamarina Hotel**, Guánica ☎ 821-0505; **Westin Río Mar Beach Resort**, Río Grande ☎ 888-8815; **Hyatt Dorado Beach** and **Hyatt Regency Cerromar Beach Hotels**, Dorado ☎ 796-1234; **Mayagüez Hilton** ☎ 831-7575; **Palmas del Mar Resort** in Humacao ☎ 852-6000, **Parador Guajataca** in Quebradillas ☎ 895-3070; **Parador Villa Antonio**, Rincón ☎ 823-2645; and **Punta Borinquen**, Aguadilla (no phone).

Many of the courts are floodlit, and if newly arrived on the island, book a court early in the morning, late in the afternoon or in the evening when it is cooler until you acclimatize to the heat.

Water Sports

The splendid 272 miles (438km) of beaches, coastline and warm clear waters offer unrivalled opportunities for a huge range of water sports, which are available at all resorts and most large hotels. There is year-round surfing, although the waves tend to be higher and rough during the winter months, with the main season extending from October to April. The World Championships were held in Rincón in 1968 and have been held there several times since. At Ramey they surf from September to April, while during the summer, the best surf is found in the southeast from Humacao south to Patillas, and especially around Punta Tuna. There is also good surfing along the north coast during the winter, including several beaches close to San Juan.

Windsurfing conditions are also good and there are conditions to suit all levels of experience, with fair winds and ocean swells along the north coast, and calmer seas on the east and southwest coasts. Again, the best conditions are during the winter when the seas run higher. Good beginner areas are the calm Condado Lagoon in San Juan, and southeast of Luquillo Beach. Isla Verde, just east of San Juan, is where many of the experienced windsurfers sail, while the most intrepid head for the northwest corner of the island and the waters off Jobos and Surfers' Beaches, and Rincón.

The Puerto Rico Water Sport Federation sets standards and guidelines for members specializing in scuba, snorkeling, sailing, deep-sea fishing, windsurfing and other aquatic activities.

TAXES

There is a 9% government tax added to all hotel bills (11% if the hotel has a casino). Some hotels also add a service charge of between 10 and 15%. Restaurants do not usually add a service charge and a tip of 15% is customary if you have enjoyed your meal. There is no sales tax but there is a 5% jewelry tax.

TELEPHONES

Puerto Rico has a modern, fiber-optics telecommunications system with direct international dialing. The international code for Puerto Rico is 787. From the US dialing Puerto Rico is a long distance call, by dialing 1-787-and the seven-digit local number. To call Puerto Rico from Britain and the rest of Europe, dial 001-787-and the seven figure local number. To call the US from Puerto Rico, dial 1 + US area code + local seven-digit number. To call any foreign country from Puerto Rico, dial 011 + country code + city code + local number.

TIME

Puerto Rico operates under Atlantic Standard Time, which is four hours behind Greenwich Mean Time and one hour ahead of Eastern Standard Time (EST) in the United States. If it is noon in London it is 8am on Puerto Rico, and when it is noon in New York, it is 1pm on the island. The island doesn't observe Daylight Savings Time, so during the summer Puerto Rico is effectively on EST, with the same time as Miami and New York.

   While it is important to know the time so that you don't miss your flight, time becomes less important the longer you stay on the island. If you order a taxi it will generally be early or arrive on time, and if you have a business meeting it will start on schedule, but for almost everything else be prepared to adopt 'Caribbean time', especially in bars, restaurants and shops. Don't confuse this relaxed attitude with laziness or rudeness, it is just the way things are done in the islands, and the quicker you accept this, the sooner you will start to relax and enjoy yourselves.

TIPPING

Tips are not generally added to bills but it is customary to tip bell-hops in hotels, taxi drivers, guides, waiters and other people providing a service. Tip taxi drivers around 10-15% and bell hops US$1-2 for each piece of luggage. Add 15% to restaurant bills if satisfied with your meal and the level of service.

TOURIST OFFICES

There are tourist information centers in:

Puerto Rico

La Princesa Building
Old San Juan PR 00901
and at Aguadilla Airport
☎ 890-3315

La Casita
Pier 1, Old San Juan
☎ 722-1709

Los Caobos Ave
Ponce
☎ 843-0465

San Juan International Airport
☎ 791-1014.

Overseas there are Puerto Rico Tourism Company offices at:

US

Florida
901 Ponce de León Boulevard,
Suite 604, Coral Gables,
Florida Fl 33134
☎ (305) 445-9112

Los Angeles
3575 West Cahuenga Boulevard,
Suite 560, Los Angeles
CA 90068
☎ (213) 874-5991

New York
666 Fifth Avenue, New York
NY 10103
☎ (212) 586-6262

Canada

Toronto
41-43 Colbourne Street,
Suite 301, Toronto,
Ontario M53 1E3, Canada
☎ (416) 368-2680

France

Paris
Express Conseil, 5 Bis.
Rue De Louvre, 75001, Paris
☎ (33-1) 44-77-88-00

Germany

Wiesbaden
Abraham Lincoln Strasse 2,
65189 Wiesbaden
☎ (49-611) 977-23-12

Italy

Genoa
Giocco Viaggil, Via Dante 2/53,
15121 Genoa
☎ (39-10) 553-11-69

Mexico

Polanco
Edif Forum, Piso 19, C. Andrés
Bello #10, Col. Polanco, Mexico
D.F. 11560
☎ (525) 282-9175

Scandinavia

Stockholm
Sergat Scandinavia,
Kammakargatan 41, S-111 24,
Stockholm, Sweden
☎ (46-8) 115495

Spain

Madrid
C/Serrano 1, 2 Izq., 28001
Madrid
☎ (34-1) 431-21-28

UK

London
67-79 Whitfield Street, London
W1P 5RL, UK
☎ 171-436-4060

WEDDINGS

Many visiting couples marry in Puerto Rico and the legal requirements, while sounding quite daunting, are not at all complicated. US citizens need identification such as a driver's license, while non-US citizens require a passport. You need to obtain the marriage license papers that can be obtained either in person, or in writing from the Department of Health, Demographic Registry Office, Box 11854, Fernández Juncos Station, Santurce, Puerto Rico PR 00910. If applying by letter, allow at least two months.
Once you have received the papers and filled them in, you must take them to a doctor on the island and obtain a medical certificate

together with a VDRL blood test. The blood test must be carried out within ten days of the wedding. Then with your ID, papers, blood test results and medical certificate, you visit the Marriage License Bureau to have all the documents authenticated. If you have been married before, a certified copy of the divorce decree or death certificate is required.

Once your papers have been authenticated, you can get married either at the free weekly Judicial Center ceremony, or at a private ceremony that will cost between $150-300.

Many hotels offer wedding and honeymoon packages and will make all the arrangements for you.

YACHTS AND MARINAS

The offshore waters attract yachts from around the world and offer excellent year-round good sailing conditions. Winds average 10-15 knots and vessels can be chartered, both crewed and bare board, for half day trips or cruises of a week and longer. The main sailing centers are San Juan, Ponce and Fajardo.

The most important event in the sailing calendar is the Discover the Caribbean Series, which takes place in September and October, and attracts a large international field.

There are marinas at:

Cangrejos Yacht Club
☎ 791-1015

Club Deportivo del Oeste
☎ 851-8880

Club Náutico de Arecibo
☎ 878-8465

Club Náutico Guayama
☎ 866-3162

Club Náutico, San Juan
☎ 722-0177

Club Náutico de Boqueron
☎ 851-1336

Club Náutico Parguera
☎ 899-5590

Club Náutico Rincon
☎ 823-8800

Club Náutico Vega Baja
☎ 858-7656

Marina del Conquistador
☎ 863-1000

Marina de Palmas, Humacao
☎ 850-2065

Marina de Salinas, Salinas
☎ 752-8484

**Ponce Yacht Club
and Fishing Club**
☎ 842-9003

Puerto Chico Marina, Fajardo
☎863-0834

Puerto Del Rey, Fajardo
☎ 860-1000

San Juan Bay Marina, San Juan
☎ 721-8062

Sea Lovers Marina
☎ 863-3762

Villa Marina, Fajardo
☎ 863-5131

Wyndham El Conquistador
☎ 863-6594

Yachts, motorboats and fishing boats are available for charter for sailing, sightseeing, fishing and diving, and longer trips.

Index

Index